Real-Life Marriage

Real-Life Marriage

NAVIGATING YOUR BEAUTIFUL, MESSY, ONE-OF-A-KIND LOVE STORY

TRACI MORROW

BROWN BOOKS
PUBLISHING GROUP

Real-Life Marriage
Navigating Your Beautiful, Messy, One-of-a-kind Love Story

Brown Books Publishing Group
Dallas, TX / New York, NY
www.BrownBooks.com
(972) 381-0009

A New Era in Publishing®

Publisher's Cataloging-In-Publication Data

Names: Morrow, Traci, author.
Title: Real-life marriage : navigating your beautiful, messy, one-of-a-kind love
    story / Traci Morrow.
Description: Dallas, TX ; New York, NY : Brown Books Publishing Group, [2022]
Identifiers: ISBN 9781612545493 (hardcover)
Subjects: LCSH: Marriage. | Interpersonal relations. | Communication in
    marriage. | Marital conflict.
Classification: LCC HQ734 .M67 2022 | DDC 646.7/82--dc23

ISBN 978-1-61254-549-3
LCCN 2021922516

Printed in the United States
10 9 8 7 6 5 4 3 2 1

For more information or to contact the author, please go to www.TraciMorrow.com.

To KC Morrow

Our story is my favorite—you are my favorite!

XOX

Table of Contents

Foreword

Dear Reader,

Traci and I are just beginning the thirty-second year of our marriage. When we were first married, we had no idea or even a thought on how our differing personalities, quirks, and habits would merge and incorporate into our relationship. Soon, as all married couples come to understand, we were challenged with these new additions, and so began our navigation of understanding the depth of marriage.

Without a guide or tools, we moved along and learned how to traverse our differences that only being in a real-life marriage can reveal. It was not always easy, and we did struggle quite a bit in the early years and, truthfully, a little beyond that. But our commitment and love for each other never wavered—we were always committed to creating a great lifelong story with each other. And through it all, we've gathered some great lessons and tools that can help anyone else who wants this too.

Among Traci's giftings is her ability to communicate her observations so clearly. She has taken the lessons and tools we have gathered throughout our marriage and put them in this book to give you hope, encouragement, and excitement that your marriage can be lifelong.

Whether you are about to be married, recently married, or long-time married, Traci has written this book for you. Jump in, and you will see hopeful new possibilities open up for your marriage.

—KC Morrow

Acknowledgments

To my dear mom and dad, Ray and Dianne Crawford: two kids who made a promise at age eighteen and have spent the last sixty-three years (and counting) creating a legacy of following Jesus, loving people, and prioritizing marriage and family. I am so blessed to be your daughter.

To my one and only sissy and brother-in-law Terri and Joe La Brie. Thanks for giving our marriage and family the best shot at making it by your example, love, and support. You stood by our sides at the altar, and then for a lifetime. KC and I are so grateful for all of it.

For my maternal grandparents Lou and Ann Taucher, married seventy-two years. You created a legacy of family that I've not seen elsewhere. Grandma, I think often of little three-year-old you: an only child who craved siblings, but lost your mama way too soon. I wonder if you look down from Heaven, see the rich depth of lifelong marriage, child bearing, adopting, and celebration of family that goes on in your people to this day, and beam with satisfaction. Every one of us in your lineage are the ginormous legacy of you and Grandpa's marriage.

For my paternal grandparents Ray and Irene Crawford, married fifty-five years. You served your community, your church, and your family with smiles, humor, humility, and a twinkle in your eyes. Grandpa, your Jesus story is one of my favorites because you invited him into your heart at age eighty-five. You lived a kind and soft-spoken life, privately carrying the unnecessary burden and inaccurate picture of being disqualified from God's love because of your humanity.

You laid down a heavy load when you accepted the saving redemption offered to you from a Jesus who loves and saves. Your story impacted mine powerfully; reminding me that it's never too late to lay down your burdens, pick up your cross, and joyfully follow Jesus.

For Lorie Pope Pauly, who prayed over me one day when I was in my thirties, seeing a vision of me writing for, speaking to, and helping people. Thanks for watering a seed by sharing that glimpse from God.

Inexpressible thanks to my mentor and friend John Maxwell. You wrote books on leadership that helped me lead myself and my family. Without your books and friendship, my path would have been far more difficult to navigate. Your books continue to guide me to create the life I intentionally choose. I pray my life follows your example in leading others to create a life they desire for themselves. I am legs to your legacy.

Special thanks to my friend Tom Reale, president of Brown books, who called me up one day and asked me to consider writing a book. Thanks for seeing a story in me to be told, friend.

Heartfelt thanks to Hallie Raymond, my editor. You helped me take my story and connect the pieces so it flowed. Thanks for speaking truthfully to me and for learning to speak my love language to encourage me.

To my readers: I pray this book illuminates the path for your marriage, and that you in turn light the way for others. I truly believe the way to positive change in our world is through individual healthy, loving marriages that go the distance. I'm FOR your one-of-a-kind love story!

Introduction

*What is "happily ever after"? Real love is a beautiful,
messy, complicated story of two imperfect people
merging their lives together, for life.*

It's been thirty-one years since I put on my big, white cream puff of a dress; unloaded a can of hairspray to make my bangs stand at attention; and walked down the aisle to my handsome groom in his tuxedo tails and mini mullet. I've learned some things. A lot of things, actually, about myself and about what it actually takes to create a marriage that goes the distance. I don't have a guarantee for a fail-proof marriage (wouldn't that be cool?), but I have discovered amazing tools that have helped us navigate the path between what we hoped marriage would be and what marriage actually looks like. These are tools that anyone can use—tools that can help you too.

Married for life. It sounds so great, doesn't it? I don't mean married in title alone, grunting it out and tolerating one another. I'm talking about the kind of marriage that goes the distance. I bet you want to like *and* love your spouse. I know I do! You want a friendship and a romance. You want great memories and adventures—maybe that includes raising kids and being grandparents together, traveling the world together, or making a house into your dream home. What's on your want list?

In my first ten or so years of marriage to my husband KC, I would never have imagined that I'd someday write about marriage.

1

Communication was so much work for us in the beginning. That's part of the beauty of growth! If you do the hard work with the person you chose, the reward is that you both grow, and it gets really good. I found something that's real and that works, and I want to share it with as many people as possible, so they too have a fighting chance in their marriages!

A much younger version of me had romantic notions of what marriage would be. Now, as an older woman who's been a wife for longer than she's been single, I want to be as real with you as possible. Marriage does, in fact, have wonderful romantic moments. But marriage can become so much more. In a marriage that goes the distance, there is a deeper intimacy than you can find in any other relationship.

When I started to use the tools I'm going to share with you in this book, they felt counterintuitive and awkward. Sometimes I'd rather have thrown them at KC when we clashed, instead of choosing to use them to build the bridge back to him. Yet, as we stopped competing against one another and started to figure out how to complement each other in our differences, our odds of succeeding in our marriage increased. I don't know what our odds actually were, but they got better—trust me.

I think it's safe to say that those of us who choose to commit to become husband and wife desire to do marriage well. The problem for most of us is that gap. You know, the one between what we dream of, see in movies, and read about in books—and the reality of creating a healthy, growing family out of two uniquely wired people raised in two different (sometimes very different) environments. I believe it's simultaneously the hardest and most rewarding thing to do well.

Do you believe it's possible to have a marriage that lasts for life? One where both of your needs are met, you're both fulfilled, and at the end, you're both glad you stayed together? Maybe you're not sure because you've rarely or never seen it firsthand in your life experience.

But I can tell you, it does exist. It is possible for you. I've seen it up close in my own family for generations. Throughout the course of my lifetime, I've witnessed the deepening relationship of two people who continued to work at their marriage and make choices to stay when things got hard.

At times in both my marriage and the successful marriages I've witnessed over the years, I've seen when growth spurts of one partner reveal lack of growth in the other. Yet they both stayed, and they fought for one another even as they fought with one another. There was nothing special or unique about the individuals in these marriages that made them more apt to make their marriage last for a lifetime—other than they believed in marriage for life, and they were willing to fight to not only make it last but make sure both partners thrived.

I've witnessed this pattern in the marriages of numerous couples my husband KC and I have mentored, in addition to seeing it in my own marriage and in the marriages of my family members. I've seen how couples work through challenges and come out stronger together on the other side. That's why I chose to write this. For you. To share what I've seen work.

The Fairy Tale Trap

From the time we are very little, we are conditioned to expect the words "and they lived happily ever after" at the end of a good story. Ask any person engaged to be married, and they most likely dream of a happily ever after once the shoe fits, the kiss wakes her, or the wedding happens. And it's not just fairy tales. We humans love a good story. In the US alone, there are between 600,000 and 1,000,000 books published annually, and about 500 to 600 movies released.[1] The majority of these fictional stories end happily. That's what we all want, isn't it?

I wonder when it was that we started packaging life to have a perfect ending "ever after." When we go to a movie or pick up a book, it's to escape reality for a while, to get lost in an entertaining fantasy world. But if we're not careful, we can become trapped in the illusion our reality-escape stories paint for us.

I want you to know right from the start that this book is not about trying to find your happily ever after. Marriage is not a fairytale, but it can be the adventure we always hoped it could be when approached with the right mindset and openness to living a *great* story. My goal is to help you navigate the beautiful, messy, complicated, real-life story that begins after you ride off into the sunset on your wedding day. The one where you get lost, or your spouse falls off the horse, or you realize that it's expensive to pay a castle's electricity. Real life stuff. Even those who live great stories experience both the highs and lows of living in a real and messy world. After "I do," we should be looking forward to the adventure that awaits us, ready to face all of what life throws at us, with our chosen partner, as we build our own great story!

My husband KC and I weren't married more than a couple of hours before we had our first happily-ever-after-shattering dispute as husband and wife. Yes. On our wedding night we got into an argument. Two in fact. The first two of many in the years to follow. They were silly and based on nothing really important, but it was eye-opening for us to realize that our marriage was going to take work if we wanted to make it good—a lot of work if we wanted to make it great. Since then, we've both made countless choices to rise to the challenge.

Anything that's worth doing is worth doing well, and that's what this book is about: navigating a marriage that goes the distance, starting with a mind shift, a plan, and behaviors to match the shift.

No matter what your childhood looked like, I don't know of any child who grows up hoping they're going to live an average life.

We want purpose. Adventure! Love. Plot twists. And for all of it to mean something. But for that to happen, outside of the movies, we need to work for it.

We want purpose. Adventure! Love. Plot twists. And for all of it to mean something.

When Two Worlds Collide

Do you have an idea of what the ideal marriage and family looks like in your mind? Some of us had a good example of family from childhood, and others dreamt of a family that would make up for what they missed growing up. Though we might have an ideal picture of what we'd like our own marriage and family to look like, we may not know how to create that with our spouse. Creating a healthy, lasting marriage and family is a pretty tall order, when you think about it. Two people raised in two different families, with sometimes radically different ways of doing things, merge together because they're attracted to one another, have fun together, and have fallen in love and chosen to get married. They then set out to create a new family with new house rules, traditions, family culture, and—if they want to have kids—to raise up the next generation of world changers. Why do we think we can do this without a lot of work and effort?

Chiseling out a lifelong, healthy, forgiving, passionate marriage, as well as a deep family culture, is the hardest thing I've ever done. It's also the most amazing thing I've been a part of creating. Having a long-term marriage has not been without hurt, forgiveness, and moments when, honestly, I was tempted to throw in the towel. If you're currently struggling in your marriage, you may look at another couple and think they must be blessed with a more cohesive pairing than you and your partner have; that other couple has something that's not available to you. If you feel that way, you are far from alone.

There are a great many people who are struggling to keep their marriages and families together and have found that *it's hard*. I know that firsthand. It's been very hard at times for us to make the marriage and family relationships that we have today. But I can assure you it is worth the effort, and it does get easier.

That's easy for me to *say*, right? I'm picturing the faces and remembering all the times over the years people have said to me, "I need to see how it works."

One night not long ago, I woke up with insomnia, and I started praying as I typically do if I can't fall right back to sleep. After nearly three hours of lying there, I got up, put on my glasses and a sweatshirt, and quietly crept out to the dining room so as not to wake KC and the kids. I grabbed a pen and legal pad and began to write about this very topic, which was weighing on my mind. A pattern began to emerge: there were a handful of principles that KC and I had faithfully applied over the years of our marriage without even realizing it. Through example and trial and error, we figured out a process of identifying and working through each issue as it came along, but we never realized it was a formula of sorts.

It's actually a simple process, a guide that enabled us to identify where we were going, why we wanted to get there, and to bring us both on board for a commonly desired outcome. But the process does take practice and patience to become good at applying it. In the early years, it took us longer to move through these steps and to find a respectful rhythm that served us both. But with experience, it has become more natural, and therefore easier, and I'm excited to share with you what has worked for us in hopes that it can add value for you as well.

Before I dive into what we've learned, let me share with you a bit of our story. You may identify with one of us, or you may just see how, glaringly, we are two different people from different backgrounds who are working hard to make our marriage a success. As of this writing, KC and I have been married for thirty-one years. We have six kids aged sixteen to twenty-eight—three boys and three girls, one adored son-in-law, a soon-to-be son-in-law, and a grandson that has our hearts wrapped around his chubby little finger. As we've raised our family and built our professions and businesses, a common topic of conversation among ourselves and others is marriage, family, and how to do these well.

I come from a family where marriage has often been highly regarded and successful for a lifetime, through multiple generations. My maternal grandparents were married seventy-two years before my mom's dad passed away in his nineties, and my paternal grandparents were married fifty-five years before my dad's dad passed away. My own parents have been married for sixty-three years as of this writing, and my siblings have had similar marriages. My sister has been married for forty-one years, and my younger brother and his bride said "I do" twenty-six years ago.

When we were growing up, my dad worked his career, plus additional seasonal jobs while going to college to get his PhD. Mom stayed at home to care for me and my four siblings, and she loved her role as a homemaker. With joy, she ran our family in the same way any passion-inspired CEO would run a business: she was intentional, creative, focused, attentive, present emotionally and physically, more than capable in a variety of areas, and financially shrewd. She purposely and passionately created a safe place and a family culture where five individuals were raised to love both God and people and to live with purpose, passion, and responsibility. We were deeply loved and supported, and my parents were (and still are) in love at eighty-two years old.

In the 1970s, our family structure was considered the norm more than it would be now. I remember that most of the moms on our cul-de-sac were homemakers. My mom walked me and my younger brother to and from the bus stop every day, we ate family breakfast every morning, family dinner every night, and both of my parents were at all of my and my siblings' sporting and school events. I can't remember seeing my parents openly argue as a child, as they chose to do so privately. My siblings and I were taught to apologize and extend forgiveness to one another. I was raised to be actively involved in church, and we prayed before meals and at bedtime. I remember even as a small girl feeling proud of my family.

We lived close to my paternal grandparents and my dad's siblings and their families. They were a part of our regular day-to-day living, coming to sporting events or coming over for dinner. My maternal grandparents lived a rowdy six-hour car ride away. My mom was one of nine children, most of whom married and scattered all over the western US but gathered together at least once a year. I have many aunts, uncles, and cousins coming from the marriage of those two precious people (there are, as of this writing, more than 160 of us on my mother's side of the family!). For as long as I can remember, family reunions were the most fun, lively memories. To this day, it feels like a small city when we all gather together. I have a cousin who used to call it "pandemonium," and chaos it was and is, but in the best of ways. As a child, I loved being a part of it so much that I couldn't help but want to have a big family to continue that familiar family dynamic.

I was fortunate to grow up surrounded by many examples of married couples who illuminated a clear path of how to intentionally create a healthy marriage and family. I'm not talking about families that act like the Brady Bunch, where everyone expects sitcom perfection, but where the family unit is thriving and husband/wife roles are both modern and timeless; a family where the kids have high expectations for their futures and from the world; where family is safe, a training ground for launching into adulthood with confidence and security.

My husband KC had a very different upbringing. He was raised by two parents who struggled to find fulfillment in their marriage. They both worked outside the home for long hours from the time he was a small boy. He was what was commonly known as a "latch-key kid" back in the 60s and 70s; he went home after school each day to let himself and his younger sister in to an empty house with no adult supervision while his parents were at work. Most of his life lessons came from his experiencing life, figuring things out through his own childhood filter. He didn't have much guidance or input from adults. He signed himself up for the sports he wanted to participate in, rode his bike to and from school, and can vividly remember the only time his dad came to see one of his sporting events. His performance wasn't discussed afterward. Not a single compliment was given.

KC loved his parents, but he remembers being scared of his dad and intimidated by his strong, opinionated mom. He has memories of hiding up in his closet while his parents fought downstairs after they drank too much, yelling at one another and throwing things; then the silence in the days that followed as no one discussed it. "I'm sorry" was never said, and forgiveness was never extended. Past issues were swept under the carpet until they were dragged back out again as ammunition during the next argument. KC's mom was openly antagonistic regarding organized religion, understandably, because she'd been wounded by words spoken by people within the church. KC was not allowed to go to church when invited by friends. Occasionally, he was permitted to attend church with his maternal grandma, but nothing was ever explained to him about the religious ceremonies he experienced.

Can you think of two more opposite childhoods? But these two worlds collided when KC and I merged as husband and wife back in October of 1990. When we brought our individual family histories to make a new family, the odds were stacked against us. Come to think of it, I think it was amazing that we lasted three hours before our first married spat! To add to our statistics, KC had already been through a painful divorce by the age of twenty-nine years old. Any gambler would not have been off to bet against us. They'd have been right to say we were a high risk, but they would have been wrong if they'd advised us not to marry. After all the work we did to strengthen the way we interacted with one another, KC and I ended up being the best thing for each other.

We had an uphill battle, but when we said "I do" to one another and to God, we were saying yes to all of it. The good, the bad, and the ugly; we had all three. If we can make our marriage last and say without hesitation it was worth it and wonderful—even when it was painful and sometimes took everything we had to protect and preserve it—then you can too. It won't be easy, but it will be worth it.

Discovering the 5 Cs

KC and I are not two perfect people who just happened to find one another. We have not created something unattainable to the average person. We are two very normal humans who, through trial, error, and learning from others together, broke down the "how-tos" of having a lasting marriage and a healthy family life. I call them the 5 Cs.

Not surprisingly, KC and I are wired completely opposite. Because of that, the way I express myself is not how he expresses himself. I highly value his input, and as I have written this book, he has weighed in with his thoughts and viewpoints to make it well-rounded, much as he does when we mentor other couples. It took two of us to create this beautiful, messy story of ours, so as you read, you'll see things that come from both of us. This book is a love offering. A collaborative effort from our very different personalities and viewpoints that make up our own one-of-a-kind marriage. We only get one life, and I want us all to live our own great love story!

KC and I didn't set out to follow any strategy. We struggled our way through, and it was only in hindsight that I began to identify a pattern: a pattern of simple yet powerful tools that work together and build off one another to create a solid marriage. These tools are the result of years of personal experience, reading books, mentoring others, getting input from others, and having the desire to not only stay away from divorce, but to have a healthy, growing, fun, and fulfilling marriage.

> If you aren't careful to grow forward together, as you grow individually, the marriage can start to suffer.

Author Peter Velander puts it this way: "If your relationship with your partner remains alive, it will look different one year, five years, and ten years from now than it does today. Living things grow and change."[2] KC and I didn't know it back when we started, but not only would we grow and change over the years, our marriage would as well. If you and your spouse aren't careful to grow forward together as you grow individually, your marriage can start to suffer. Every couple consists of separate human beings with different gifts, talents, viewpoints, interests, personalities, and methods of doing even the simplest things. But in marriage you become one—one living, breathing organism involving two human beings. That one marriage has two partners who both need to make the relationship a priority, sometimes fighting like mad against culture and habits to keep it alive and growing in a healthy manner.

These 5 Cs can help you. When you implement them consistently, they can become second nature and help you navigate even the toughest challenges through self-awareness and clear, healthy communication. I'll present them to you now, and then we'll break each one down in a separate chapter with steps for how you can immediately begin applying what you learn.

The 5 Cs

1. **Choose** your desired outcome. Identify your priorities and what you envision in the long run as you grow in your relationship.

2. **Communicate** clearly what you desire. People express themselves differently, so this can be the hardest tool to master, but it can also be the one with the biggest return. Clear communication has the power to unlock intimacy and trust as you learn to share your thoughts, feelings, and desires within the safe boundaries of a commitment for life.

3. **Collaborate** on a plan or method to make your marriage work. Although ideas and thoughts are great, without a plan of action with clearly outlined steps, they're ineffective. The two of you need a clearly defined way of moving forward toward what you truly and deeply desire for your marriage.

4. **Commit** to the process. Building a healthy relationship is a long game. It takes intentional effort over a lifetime to develop healthy, regular communication; marriage is a big, important thing you're committing to.

5. **Check in** regularly to make sure the plan is still agreeable and working. This step can sometimes come out in the form of an argument, as anything that's not bringing about results can cause us to feel frustrated. I'll give you some suggestions for how to keep this step from derailing your process!

It takes a lifetime to create a healthy partnership, and after reading this book you'll have identified what you really want for and from your marriage, and you'll have the tools to help you follow through on making those goals a reality. And the beauty is, as you get better at the relationships in your home, your relationships outside of your home and family will naturally get better as well. The 5 Cs can become a part of how you interact and relate with everyone, not just your spouse.

One of the things I learned through my own journey was that the sooner I applied what I'd learned, the more apt I was to apply it at all. That's why I'd suggest you take action on what you learn as you're reading, if possible. It won't be perfect right out of the gate, and sometimes it will feel awkward; applying new ways of doing life and relationships generally does. But rather than trying to perfect in your head what you will do, it's best to just start.

Before we go further, let me be clear: defining the 5 Cs, or even living by them, will not make life turn out exactly as planned. We have to be creative as life unfolds and the unexpected happens; that's part of the adventure! But with a plan you both agree to, revisit often, and revise when necessary, and with hard work from both partners, you can create the marriage you both desire.

It's often said that, "Life is what happens when you've got something else planned." Let me help you set an expectation at the start: you'll need to stay flexible. As important as it is to have a plan in place, you'll need to mentally commit to purposely navigate through the unexpected and to follow through as you adjust your plan to fit your life. A marriage for life will require creative tenacity from you as you execute your plan to address what's happening now versus what you ultimately want to happen in the long term. There are things in culture that will work against you as you set out on your quest for a lifelong marriage—things that could derail your plans and desired outcomes. There will be times, when you are weary or tired, when advice and cultural influences will appeal to you. But nothing is as rewarding and fulfilling as fighting against all of these things to create a lasting, thriving marriage and family.

As we raise a toast to the bride and groom, let's also commit to the process of navigating a lifelong marriage!

Chapter
1

Begin with Buy-In

"All's well that begins well."[3]
—John C. Maxwell

If you want your marriage to become a great story, there are a few things I want to share and suggest upfront. Before you add the 5 Cs to your marriage toolbox, your first step should be to state your intentions to your spouse or future spouse. You don't have to have the perfect words, but it's important for you and your partner to be on the same page; it's important to have buy-in from both of you.

If you're like KC and me, these discussions will happen many times throughout the years, ensuring things are working for both of you and remembering that you're on the same team. Talk about what you want for yourself, your marriage, and your family. How you begin the conversation is important. You can end the conversation just as quickly as you start it and shut down progress if you put your partner on the defense to start. Eliminate sentences starting with "you." For example, "You are so negative all the time," "You are so frustrating," "You never . . . ," or "You always . . . ," and so on. You want to start this discussion off in a positive way!

Put yourself in your significant other's shoes. Depending on how well you've communicated up to this point, your partner might not know why you want to change the way things are working. People resist change, even healthy change. Change is scary. It's unknown. We may feel defensive. It takes work, and if you haven't been in the habit of working on your relationship in this way, this can seem daunting or as if it's coming from out of left field. That's why it's important that you remove distractions and begin any conversation about working on your marriage by stating how much you care for your spouse and your relationship. Stating your intentions for yourself is also important. Clearly, lovingly, and even excitedly state that your intentions are to move forward in a different way, together, as a team, in order to make things the best they can be. Tell your partner that you've found a book that will help you create a marriage that is ideal for both of you, and ask if they are willing to read with you and be an active part of the process. Say you are starting with self examination and that you'd like to go through this process together. Admit that you don't know all that the process will involve, but you want to read the book together and discuss what you're reading.

Not all couples will interact with this book in the same way. If your spouse or significant other is onboard and willing to read along with you from the start, then your interaction with the steps will come as a result of individually reading and then discussing what you're learning and how you see the 5 Cs being applied in your relationship. If your spouse is defensive from the start or not open to going through a book together, you could perhaps make the agreement that you will read the first couple of chapters and then share what you're learning on a prearranged date night that you can schedule to discuss your relationship. There isn't a right way, as long as you are both willing to go through the steps presented here.

There are a variety of reasons your spouse might not be open to this exercise at first. Your spouse may not be a reader, or they may not have witnessed what it looks like to work on a marriage intentionally. Beginning to operate within your relationship differently might feel intimidating or threatening, depending on your spouse's background and personality. Still others might think the marriage is good enough, or have an "if it ain't broke, don't fix it" mentality. Wherever your partner is, when you approach them about going through this book and working on your relationship, the goal is to be positive, not to attack them if your initial conversation doesn't go exactly as planned. Work together on how to best approach the 5 Cs in a way that makes both of you comfortable. Don't lead with an attitude that suggests, "This is broken. Let me help you fix you."

Be safe, be kind, be vulnerable, and be patient. Trust that while even getting your spouse to discuss this process may be a big step at first, it will be worth it to get the conversation going. That can be a pretty big hurdle, but once the door is open, it's just a matter of learning how to navigate the conversation. KC isn't really a big reader, so many of our conversations start with my sharing what I'm learning, and his engaging verbally with me. This is just one way of opening the conversation. Every couple is different. If your partner doesn't want to work through this book with you at first, my best advice is to read it through yourself. Interact with the 5 Cs alone, letting the process work in you. Then, share what you are learning (not what you might feel your spouse needs to learn) in such a way that is disarming but engaging. It might be a process, and that's okay. Every marriage is unique, so find what works for you.

I know a few couples who communicated brilliantly right from the start, and to you I say, what a head start! That makes declaring the need to work on your marriage much easier and more natural, and though you will still have to work through things, it's great to have the wind at your back. For the rest of us, it takes time to get to the starting line of a conversation about working on our marriages. I can remember when KC and I first had this kind of conversation. I think we'd been married for fifteen years and had already spent many years figuring one another out. Don't get me wrong. We'd had a lot of conversations about how we could make things better over the years and as we were raising our family, but this conversation was different. It stood out because it finally felt like we really understood one another enough to make a declaration for the next phase of our marriage: a mature, next-level discussion. If you are starting out your marriage or are in the beginning stages and didn't have to work through as much as we did to get to a new starting line of sorts, I am so happy for you!

Marriage Mentors

It's said that you are the sum total of the five people you hang around with most. If your goal is to have a healthy, thriving marriage and family life, then you need to intentionally put yourself in a place where you are regularly around people who value and seek after the same. It's obviously more helpful if both you and your spouse or future spouse desire the same things from your marriage and family life, but if you desire different things, you're going to need some support so you can live purposefully.

I have had well-meaning, dear, sincere friends give me advice for my marriage that—though genuinely intended to be supportive— actually countered what I really wanted long-term for my marriage and life. I learned two things from this: one, a person can be sincere but sincerely wrong with their advice, and two, you can always find someone to affirm you in a decision, whether that decision is right or wrong. It's up to you to find people who will not only love and encourage you but be willing to tell you the hard things from a loving place, in support of the long-term goals you have for your marriage.

A sidenote here: this book is not about making an abusive situation healthy. Moving forward, the challenges I refer to in marriage refer only to the hardships typical of blending two different people for a lifetime. My advice pertains to two people making it work in a safe marriage relationship. If you are in an unsafe situation, please seek outside help immediately.

In the beginning, KC and I made some wise decisions that I believe are a large part of how we made it through those early years. We were both pretty new in our Christian faith, so we committed right away to premarital mentoring that was offered at our church. This was especially powerful for two people who experienced two very different ways of communicating in our families of origin. Having someone walk us through basic steps for healthy communication was invaluable, and that is why we are so passionate now about providing marriage and marriage-prep mentoring for couples today. Our premarital mentoring course took us (like we now take others) through books and workbooks on topics like communication, sexual intimacy and fidelity, family history and traditions, raising kids, how we view money, expectations of one another, and expectations of the roles of husband and wife both specifically and in general. These are all relevant topics which are really helpful for setting a couple up with healthy and accurate expectations. And if you're already married, many churches have marriage mentoring for learning these same tools, no matter how long you've been married. I also have an online digital marriage mentoring course if there isn't one live at one of your local churches.

The other thing that worked to our benefit was attending an adult Sunday school class with other newly married couples to be mentored in a group setting. Here, we met other couples who were roughly our age, were in the same stage of life, had similar desires for their marriage, and were looking to surround themselves with people with the same beliefs and values. As we figured the early days of marriage out with other couples in this class, each week, we'd hear from a different speaker brought in to strengthen and help couples looking to have healthy marriages based on core biblical values (love, respect, fidelity, joy, peace, patience, forgiveness, how to interact with our families of origin, how to navigate healthy communication, etc.). Then, we'd discuss what we heard from the speaker in smaller groups, sharing our varied responses and breaking down how to apply the lesson. This was especially helpful because, due to our individual filters, KC and I oftentimes heard different things from the same message. Here, we formed a community with other people who were like us, blending two different upbringings into one new family. This community brought accountability and people we could safely share our struggles with and show support through theirs as well. Those are really some of my favorite times as a young couple: learning how to do marriage well with new, like-minded friends who were going through the same things we were going through as newlyweds. It was a support group, and we were all in it together. Big shout out to our friends from "The Honeymooners" at Lake Avenue Congregational Church in Pasadena, California! These kinds of small groups are available to any couple, no matter their age and stage of life, through almost any local Bible-teaching church.

The third thing KC and I had was a mentor couple: people we looked up to and admired for how they conducted their marriage and family life and who were a bit further along in the journey than we were. This couple just happened to be my favorite (and only) sister Terri and brother-in-law Joe La Brie. Terri and Joe met in and dated all through college before they married at twenty-one. I was eleven at the time, and at the wedding rehearsal when all of the bridal party gathered, Joe introduced me to one of his friends from high school. I very clearly remember nodding at twenty-one-year-old KC as he sat in his chair, then avoided him the rest of the festivities because I was a kid, and he was a stranger at this gathering of people I mostly knew. I didn't see KC again until eight years later when I moved in with my sister and Joe for a year. When we met again, well, let's just say that my response to him was different as a nineteen-year-old!

Joe was a great friend and example to KC, who hadn't had another example of a man doing family life well. Joe was and is a man who values his family and his growing, active relationship with God. He also has had the unique perspective of having known me as a little sister since I was eight years old and being KC's closest friend since high school. It made him safe for both of us, and truly someone we could both trust in times when we needed outside perspective. Joe was the guy KC called one night while in the middle of his divorce. KC had watched the marriage and faith my sister and Joe had and realized the spiritual piece to his life was missing. He prayed with Joe, inviting God into his life, and thus began his own spiritual journey.

Likewise, my sister is one of the wisest women I've ever known, with a heart to pray for, support, and love people. She has been my best friend and mentor on many levels throughout my adult life.

Terri and Joe were a blessing to us, and a few times in the early days, they were the people we went to to help us work through an impasse when we'd get stuck. Like us, they aren't perfect, but they walk their talk humbly and joyfully, and they let us walk alongside them—more closely when we've needed extra help. A mentor couple is a huge part of doing life well; we all need to see someone else do it well to know that we can. If you can't think of someone you know that fits that description, keep watching for one, and in the meantime, I'm glad you picked up this book!

Whatever stage of life you're in, whether engaged, newlyweds, or married for any given amount of time, these three things are available to you: a marital mentoring class, a like-minded group of people in your same stage of life with common beliefs for accountability, and a mentor couple ahead of you in their marriage and family willing to walk through the highs and lows with you. Finding and developing a mentor couple relationship might take some time, but you can begin right away with premarital or marriage mentoring and a small group—available at many evangelistic churches. A Bible-based church is a great resource for marriage and family support. Even if you're not a particularly religious person or regular church-goer, you will be able to find a group that is pro-marriage and family and is there to support you. Ask around (preferably, ask a person whose life you admire and who appears to be emotionally healthy, humble, and growing). You may be amazed at the resources that are out there that you just didn't know about.

The Comparison Trap

A word of caution: there is a difference between looking to couples you admire as a model and a source of advice and comparing your marriage to your friends' marriages. Comparison is never healthy; it sets us up to be disappointed with what we have. When we compare our story, something we know every detail of, good and bad, to someone else's story, where we know less of the bad than of the good, our view is skewed and incomplete, and the comparison is not going to be accurate. This is a common temptation in our present world with social media playing the role it does in our relationships.

I love what my sweet sister-in-law Alisha Crawford says when she hears someone comparing: "Not your story." What a simple yet profound comment. We don't know the whole story of anyone else's marriage or relationship, and when we compare, we take all the details from a messy piece of our life that we're perhaps dissatisfied with at the moment and compare it to one small piece or picture of theirs that seems to be put together. That isn't an accurate depiction of the whole picture of either relationship. Once I stopped holding up our relationship to my sister's marriage, or my friend's marriage, I was free to appreciate our unique differences, and to value KC's "different" with joy and appreciation, not frustration. Every couple has their own struggles and just because you don't see another couple's doesn't mean they don't exist. They do. We can learn best practices from others, but comparison won't help our situation. We must learn to put on mental blinders and stop ourselves from thinking in terms of how our relationship measures against someone else's. If you find yourself doing this, remind yourself, "Not my story."

Anyone who is currently in a healthy marriage that has lasted for several years will tell you that it's to be expected that trials and conflict in a marriage will come. It's not an easy task to combine two people's personalities, backgrounds, and ways of doing things, and create one healthy, functioning family unit. It takes time to merge your lives. As you begin to build the kind of marriage you desire, there will be times when you will feel like you're not making progress, or times when you'll wonder why you keep working at this when it doesn't seem to be working for you. You may even be there right now. Maybe you're on board with change, but your spouse isn't. That's a tough position for anyone, and it can add to the weight you feel as you try to build a healthy, long-term relationship.

This book will serve as a guide for you: a guide on how to do your best with what you know and have, so you can look back with confidence on how you handled the parts you were responsible for. Set aside any unrealistic expectations of how this might look for both spouses and fully own your part; don't expect the other person to make you happy. Let me tell you right now: another person will not make you happy. That, my friend, is your own responsibility.

My life mentor and friend, a best-selling author and leadership expert, John C. Maxwell, tells a story of a time not long after his own marriage began. He was leading a group discussion on marriage with his wife, Margaret. One of the questions from the audience that day was directed to Margaret: "Margaret, does John make you happy?" John talks of how he was so excited to hear her answer, and in that split second between the question being asked and his new wife giving her answer, he envisioned all of the wonderful things she was going to say about him because, well, he knew what a wonderful husband he was.

Then Margaret answered.

"No," she said thoughtfully. "It didn't take me long in our marriage to realize that John could never make me happy."

If you know John or have ever heard him tell this story when he speaks, at this point he pauses with the most astounded, dumbfounded, wounded, "surely you misunderstood the question" expression on his face. It's a great moment with exaggerated facial expressions and body language that connects with his audience. It's relatable because we'd all hope that if our spouse was asked if we made them happy, they'd say yes!

But Margaret knew better. She went on to say, "I don't expect John to make me happy because I am the only person who is responsible for my happiness. That's not John's responsibility; it's mine."

What a powerful statement for a young bride to make, and even more so to have discovered so early in marriage! For some people this takes a lifetime, or several failed marriages, to discover. If it didn't sink in, read again what she said. Your happiness is your responsibility. Likewise, your spouse is responsible for their own happiness. When we mistakenly believe a partner will make us happy, and they don't, it makes sense to leave that person and go to the next relationship to find happiness. The problem is, if I am the one responsible for my happiness, and I leave one relationship that doesn't make me happy to head into the next, whom have I just dragged into this new relationship, without owning any responsibility? The only one who can actually change my happiness barometer is me.

> The only one who can actually change my happiness barometer is me.

Freeing Advice

Perhaps the best marriage advice I've ever been given was from my mom. It wasn't flashy; in fact, it was delivered over the phone, in the middle of a conversation that covered the grand scope of things a mother and young adult daughter cover in a weekly phone call. At the time, I didn't even know it would become what I now consider my best piece of relationship advice. The simplicity of it might surprise you. My mother said to me: "Traci, your husband will not meet all of your needs. That's why you need friends." That's it. Before you express too much disappointment at the fact that this piece of advice doesn't teach us how to attain world peace, let me assure you that the wisdom of this statement, after having implemented it for a few decades now, quite possibly could be the answer to a world of peace, beginning in individual marriages. Let me explain.

When I chose to marry KC, my mom knew that very quickly I would discover that just because KC was the man I was in love with, it didn't mean he was put on this earth to meet all of my needs. And vice versa. That message, that has brought me understanding and peace since she first spoke it, has several layers.

> It's an antiquated belief in modern times that another person completes you.

When I began thinking about my mom's advice, the unconscious burden I had been carrying, the expectation that KC would complete me, lifted from my mind. It's an antiquated belief in modern times that another person completes you, but if we're honest, don't we sort of, deep down, think that finding romantic love might fill or fix some things in our life? That once we find Mr. or Mrs. "Right" we'll feel better, be happy, feel whole? While having a lifetime partner is fulfilling, it is also challenging because that partner brings a whole new way of living and doing life into the very same living space where you have your own ways, and together you create your new norm through a million little decisions. Some of those decisions will come as a compromise you have made on former preferences, and others will come as a result of the battles you'll choose to fight. To say it's easy is both inaccurate and setting you up for failure if you believe or expect it. Don't get me wrong—it's exciting and meaningful to merge your lives together and create a new way; it just won't solve all of your problems. In fact, the relationship will most likely create new issues or highlight areas you both need to work on to be a better partner, and the temptation will be to blame one another. Just as a young Margaret Maxwell learned that her new husband wasn't responsible for her happiness, so too must we take responsibility for our own contentment—even when circumstances are difficult.

The second thing my mom's advice did for me was to remind me that I needed friends—and they needed me. Friends—in the plural. When I was young, I went through a string of best friends. I had a tendency to look to the one person who seemed a perfect fit at that time; we would spend every free moment together, were interested in the same things, and thought the same things were fun and funny. Once that younger version of me figured out that we had differences in areas, like the fit wasn't quite right anymore, I'd seek out a new best friend. When my mom gave me her advice about marriage, it reminded me that what I had learned all those years ago applied to adult life too: that one person won't meet all of your needs—each person is wonderfully made and gifted and brings their own unique something to the friendship, as will you. Every friend has a different role in your life, and you have something to bring to their lives as well. For me, this released KC from being my everything and freed me from feeling like I needed to be his. Maybe that's a no-brainer for you, and if so, be sure you share it with new brides and grooms—it's powerful! If, however, you've been expecting your spouse to meet all of your needs and make you happy, and maybe are even feeling like you married the wrong person and want to find a new one, I hope this idea frees you by expanding your thinking. Your spouse has a specific role in your life—your life partner, lover, closest ally, and safe friend—but that doesn't mean they have to like the same books or movies, laugh at the same things, like the same foods, or enjoy travel as much as you do. Your spouse will not have your exact interests, and that's okay. Friends can fill those roles and provide variety in your life at the same time.

Now, knowing this fact and actually living it are two different things. Maybe we're late bloomers, but it took KC and I a long time to really get this down. We are about as opposite as two people can be. We have the same beliefs about God, some similar interests, and a similar sense of humor, but beyond that, we are diametrically opposite on most other things. The things I'm particular about don't bother him at all, and vice versa. I love change; he thrives in routine. He likes to drive fast; I like a little safer pace. He prefers war movies; I prefer relational movies. I'm boisterous and expressive; he's quiet and contemplative. I process out loud; he processes in his head. I like to set goals and plans; he likes to live in the moment. I like a busy calendar; he likes large margins for down time. And the list goes on. After about fifteen years of marriage, and having read loads of books and personality assessments, we finally figured out that we're different! And it's okay. In fact, we found that our differences benefit us.

"Really, Traci?" you may be asking. "You needed books and assessments to figure that out?" Yes. Yes, we did. When we finally figured out that we didn't have to become more like each other, that there was no right or wrong in so many of those issues that had the potential to become big conflicts if left unaddressed, we finally were free. Free to see what all that pushing and pulling against one another

> When we let go of the "your way, my way; right way, wrong way" mentality, we discovered that we are an incredible team.

had caused us to overlook for so long: that we are actually the perfect complement to one another. When we let go of the "Your way, my way; right way, wrong way" mentality, we discovered that we are an incredible team.

Seek Out Resources for Understanding Each Other

There are so many wonderful resources today for new couples. I want to share a couple helpful books that have not only helped KC and I unlock one another's built-in code but are also foundational for the couples we mentor. These tools have been life-changing for us.

The first is *Personality Plus* by Florence Littauer.[4] There are a lot of personality tests out there, and you may prefer another, but the one I recommend is a simple model to start with. If you search for "Personality Plus test Littauer" you can print out and take the assessment, but I really recommend reading the book to help you understand yourself and your partner. The defining of your personality types isn't meant to be used as an excuse to get out of healthy conversations—"You know I'm wired to resist conflict!"—but rather as a tool to help you understand your own and your partner's strengths and weaknesses as you work to mesh your lives together and bring healthy communication patterns into your marriage and family.

Personality Plus changed the way we viewed, and therefore treated, one another. We read about each other's personalities on a date night, and it was mind-blowing! For the first time, we identified our individual tendancies in behavior or attitude as simply the way we each were wired to view or approach certain situations. Today, we have it marked, and tabbed, to review as needed. Once we had kids, we had them take the test, and then we read to them about themselves, their siblings, and their dad and I to better understand each other. One Christmas I printed the test for all of my siblings, their spouses, my parents, and my grown nieces and nephews. God bless them all for being willing to participate! After everyone took the test, we all had a great discussion as we all fell into our prospective personality groups. It was enlightening. It brought out hilarious stories as people began decoding themselves and one another. It was relationship-enhancing and gave us common language to refer to one another's personality aspects. I cannot recommend this step enough.

The second book that made an impact in our marriage and family is *The 5 Love Languages* by Gary Chapman.[5] This book is KC's favorite go-to book when we work with couples. Chapman shares the five common ways people express and receive love, and he includes an assessment to discover your own: acts of service, personal touch, gifts, words of affirmation, and quality time. He explains how most people give love in their own language, so if, for example, you love words of affirmation, you are going to praise and encourage people with loving words and perhaps desire it from them in return. Words of affirmation is my top love language for how I receive love. I really gush on my loved ones verbally, sharing all of my thoughts and love and appreciation for them with words. Likewise, when someone gives me a genuine word of encouragement or compliment, it's nourishment to my soul. KC's love language has morphed over the years (and this can happen to you too). His language has now become words of affirmation, but for years it was predominantly quality time. He loves to get into deep conversation while sitting down, preferably over a good meal or hot cup of coffee, one-on-one. While I enjoy deep conversation, I prefer to talk and listen while wiping down counter tops or folding a load of laundry—multitasking—rather than just sitting and talking. Can you see how this could cause each of us to feel sometimes unloved by the other in those early years? He would prefer I stop multitasking long enough to sit down and engage with him—and without falling asleep. Back before *The 5 Love Languages*, my mind wasn't wired to slow down enough to simply sit and talk, and I didn't know enough to just do it anyway because it's what my husband needed. We went a lot of years, I'm sorry to say, where we were loving one another in totally different languages, and for a long time both of us felt that the other wasn't giving their best.

While we were loving one another in the way that came most natural to us, we were missing one another's expression of that love. Our example proves the value of books like these and the importance of not just reading them, but making the ideas a part of ourselves through implementation. Consistently. They are tools to help us understand that we are created differently, and when we understand ourselves and one another, relationships deepen, needs are met, and we can focus on other things rather than our empty emotional cup. When KC read *The 5 Love Languages*, he said, "For the first time I really got what you were saying. Before I thought you were just asking me for what you wanted, but after the book I realized it was how you're wired; that it's not just what you want but what you *need*. I didn't understand before that loving you in the way you best receive it was like oxygen to your soul." The more you understand yourself and your partner and how they give and receive love, the more you can really speak to them in their love language, and, in so doing, powerfully communicate your love for them in the way they receive it best.

The Power of Forgiveness

One way we can show love to someone is through forgiveness. A lifelong marriage will require a lot of forgiveness; of yourself and of your spouse. Early in my marriage, I was surprised when a dear friend said she'd never heard that an appropriate response to when someone says "I'm sorry" is "I forgive you." I had never heard of another response.

"What do you say?" I asked her, stunned.

"I just say 'it's okay' or 'thank you,'" she answered.

Since then, we've asked couples we've mentored the same question, and most say what my friend said. This may be a major difference between you and your spouse as well, but setting this boundary on forgiveness is critical to healthy relationships. We decided that "I forgive you" was how we'd respond when we apologized to one another. Saying "it's okay" didn't always ring true in the moment because, oftentimes, the situation wasn't okay. The words, the action, or the misunderstanding hurt; the act of forgiving says we both agree that, whether intentionally or not, one person has hurt the other and is sorry, and the other forgives and releases any grudges they might hold.

If you have offended your spouse and have given them a sincere apology, they might not be ready to forgive you. This has happened more times than I can count in our marriage. When I learn that I've offended KC, and I hear how it made him feel, I was (and am) typically quick to sincerely apologize. I really love a fast resolution; but to be fair, it's not anything I work on. It's just how I'm wired. I also do my best in an argument to consciously, purposely remember that I am for KC and for our marriage. My core belief is that individual situations of annoyance, misunderstanding, or misinterpretation are worth less than my overall desire to have a great marriage. Even when I'm really offended or mad, my goal is never to hurt KC intentionally; it's always for mutual understanding and the restoration of our relationship. When I say I'm sorry, I mean it, because what I want overall is more important than most situations of conflict. That's something that's decided in my mind. Any situation that pops up is never greater than my overall goal.

KC has learned to do this as well, but it took him a while because it wasn't taught or modeled in his home. In the early days of our marriage, he needed time to cool down and let his emotions calm, so he could think clearly and get back to that same base: the overall health and restoration of the relationship. We have never been name-callers, but I do know that is a common coping habit that some people have. It is just that: a habit that is counterproductive and can be unlearned. As a couple, you can choose to address this unproductive and unhealthy pattern, preferably not in the middle of a disagreement, and together commit to stick to the individual issue and not to exacerbate it by calling names or titling behavior. Become intentional about not putting labels or names on one another. It's an unnecessary, hurtful distraction from the topic at hand, and in the end, it becomes one more thing to apologize for as you heal. Navigating the creation of new, healthier habits will take a lot of time; it did for us, anyway. If you've been name-calling for years, titling behavior, or using any other unfair fighting technique, it may take years to undo. In our situation, learning to refocus on our relationship couldn't have happened faster for me, but KC had to change habits that were deeply rooted in his childhood. In my experience, conscious choices to undo unhealthy lifelong patterns and habits that have become second nature may take a lifetime. You have to want to fix the habits because, though saying you want to change is simple enough, making the change a part of you takes time. And isn't that a big piece of what marriage is as well? Choosing to work it out with one person for your whole life? What other relationship do you have like that? Marriage really is a very special and unique relationship.

> Saying you want to change a habit is simple enough, making it a part of you takes time.

In the early years, after KC took time to cool off in order to process and forgive, we would then clarify what one had said in an argument, what the other person heard, and what was actually meant.

Saying "I'm sorry" and "I forgive you" are a healthy part of resolution, but sometimes you need to talk out what was said and what was heard for the sake of resolution—and so as not to repeat old patterns. Most miscommunications happen because what you thought you were communicating was not at all what the other person heard. That's where our marriage prep counseling exercise comes in.

Let me illustrate an argument from our early years' archives. One night, early in our marriage, KC and I were going out on a date after work. I spent time picking out my clothes. When I walked out from the bedroom, ready to go out to dinner, KC noticed my capri pants and said jokingly, "Why didn't you pay the extra ten bucks and get the whole pant?"

I went back to my room and changed. I was embarrassed. My feelings were hurt. Without asking my husband, I assumed three things: that he thought I looked silly, that he had said so in order to offend me, and that the correct course for him now was to follow me and apologize for what he had said. But he didn't follow me or apologize. He just went about his business, clueless that I was offended. I got very silent and eventually was stomping around the house. Still, he had no clue. I was so mad and even angrier because he hadn't noticed I was pouting. Finally, I confronted him.

"I am so mad at you!" I said. "Not only did you not say anything nice to me when I came out ready to go, but you made fun of my clothes. You made me feel terrible about myself, and it ruined the whole night for me! And now you sit there like you didn't do anything wrong!"

KC's face: deer in the headlights.

I'm sure you're probably much more mature than I was back then, but the younger me used to make a lot of assumptions and accusations in these kinds of statements. I assumed he was making fun of me. I wrongly stated (and believed) that he had the power to make me feel bad about myself. My reaction to his comment had compounded quickly because I hadn't expressed that I was hurt right off the bat. I didn't draw a boundary.

I love the saying, "You teach people how to treat you by what you allow." I let my hurt become anger. I let it grow quickly with each passing minute. I created a whole scenario around my emotional response to his words, assigning an intention behind what he had said. I'd basically taken one offense and turned it into a whole case, mixing up my feelings with what had actually happened. Part of it was immaturity and lack of development in me, but remember—words are my love language, so a joke at the expense of twenty-one year old me without the balance of a positive word of affirmation felt far bigger than it ever needed to be. As a young, new bride I just wasn't equipped to deal with it. Eventually I learned to say, "Babe, when you said my capri pants are goofy, I felt you were telling me I looked silly, when I put time and thought into picking what I was going to wear."

If I had said something like that, KC might have said, "I was just being playful. I'm sorry I hurt your feelings. I really didn't mean anything by it." I would have in turn extended actual and verbal forgiveness. Over time, and with intentional choices, KC learned to lead with a word of encouragement or compliment rather than a joke. It's a seemingly silly example, but those little things can feel so big in a marriage.

While talking it out might be your strong suit, that may put your spouse at a disadvantage. This was how it was for us. KC needs time to process before he can properly express what he wants to say in a moment of stress. It can become a challenge when one wants time to think (maybe even a day or so, depending on the seriousness of the issue being discussed), and the other wants to deal with an issue immediately and move on. I give KC huge props—he grew up surrounded by examples that did not show how to have a healthy marital spat, and while in the early days he would revert to what he knew, he was pliable and willing to work at this for the health of our marriage. That's a huge piece to conflict resolution: wanting to learn how to make things right in a healthy way. It's hard to change old habits, but once you've decided that you want to grow, resolution is much more productive. And you can be creative in your problem-solving. Sometimes using forms of communication other than talking can help. KC quickly found while he was learning to communicate through conflict that he was much better at communicating his feelings through writing notes or letters to me. His brain allows him to process and express himself through writing much faster than he can through speaking. So, I would share my thoughts verbally, he would listen, process, and write, and then we'd discuss. Whether you talk it out, write a letter, journal, or sing, just find what helps you get to a place where you can express yourself best!

You may identify with me, or with KC, or fall somewhere in between. I want to encourage you. When you are purposeful and intentional, when you take action by practicing what you learn, and when you have a spouse who loves you, is patient with you, and remains willing to work through conflict, you can change unhealthy communication styles and learned habits from your family of origin. Figuring out the best way to communicate with your person in the safe environment of marriage will take time. The 5 Cs will help you navigate your way to a marriage you can look back on with satisfaction and fulfillment. Let's take a look at the first C.

Key Choices

- Identify couples you admire and who could be good mentors
- Choose to put on blinders: unfollow or mute social media accounts that are comparison traps for you
- Identify any areas in your relationship where you've grown complacent
- Choose to take responsibility for your own happiness

Chapter 2

Choose the Marriage You Want

"It's the start that stops most people."[6]
—Don Shula

While most people would say they want to be married for life, wanting something and actively choosing to follow through on it are two different things. The difference between those who act on what they've chosen and those who want to, but don't, comes down to a few details: having the right tools, an emotionally safe and loving environment in which to practice using those tools, and the tenacity to work for a lifetime toward a commonly desired choice with the person you promised to love, honor, and cherish for as long as you both shall live. The big question is, "Where are those tools?"

The 5 Cs are the simple, practical tools that will take you through identifying what you desire for your marriage and then making it happen. There will be large ideas and themes you'll want to dream and discuss for your marriage. Perhaps you've already touched on them up to this point—questions like where you'll live, whether you'll travel, if you desire to have children, and if so, how many? In addition to the big decisions a couple makes, there are a lifetime of many little topics that will pop up, cause a bit of friction, and reveal areas where you need to choose to do some work. You'll "choose"—the first C—many different things throughout your life as a married couple that you'll want to address head-on, with honesty, forthrightness, and lots of grace.

Create Space to Think

Healthy people in healthy relationships don't just happen. It takes work. Consistent work. From both people. And the rewards in the long-term are worth the work you put in on the front end. You need to start by intentionally creating a time and place to think about what you really want for your marriage. You've got to put that time on your calendar. Once you've scheduled the time, find a place where you are comfortable and undistracted.

If you're thinking, "Life is so busy, I don't have time, and I can't imagine a place where I'd be undistracted," as your friend with six kids, a husband, and three businesses, I am lovingly saying to you, incorrect! It's entirely possible. You may need to get creative or let some things go in your schedule—TV, the time-suck of social media scrolling, sleep, cleaning time (you're welcome!)—to make space for working on yourself and your marriage. After your relationship with your Creator, your marriage is the most important relationship in your life, so it is definitely worth creating space on your busy calendar for it.

Schedule a regular "appointment" with yourself, then pick the meeting spot. Make it a place that you'll look forward to and enjoy with as many senses as possible. I like to get up early and sit in my dining room or back deck, depending on the time of year, with a favorite mug of hot, steaming coffee. I keep a warm blanket and a comfy sweatshirt nearby if I get chilly. I like to be able to look up and think and process while looking at something peaceful and pretty; a bunny or deer browsing in my backyard, or the sun coming through the trees outside my front window. I like the quiet of morning, but I sometimes will put on classical music that I've picked ahead of time and made into a playlist. It's like my own personal retreat in the middle of a busy, full life to just think and prayerfully check in with myself and what is happening in my life. I've been doing this for years now, so while it might feel new and odd to you, you're far more apt to stick to this time if it's a pleasing experience that you look forward to.

You'll probably want to go to your spot several times as we work through this chapter because you'll be doing some deep and important thinking. Get it on your schedule and keep that appointment with yourself. Don't let yourself fall into the trap of "when I have time," because that time will likely never appear on its own. You'll have to make the time.

When you go to your thinking place, bring a notebook and pen or your tablet so you can put down your thoughts. Then put your phone on airplane mode to block out the distraction of technology. You may have to constantly redirect your thoughts and discipline your attention to stay on the matter at hand. You might pick up your phone several times out of habit to check an app you use regularly. I get it. I do it too. But I make myself stay. I remind myself that what I'm doing in that moment is far more important than checking messages, or likes, or even virtual interactions with friends and family.

Choosing the outcome you desire for your marriage will be directly related to your priorities, so if you are struggling with where to start, first take some time to identify your top priorities. If every decision we make can be run through the filter of our priorities, we will have an easier time agreeing and committing, and we'll be more motivated when things get difficult or out-and-out hard.

If you're feeling like "choose what you want" sounds so big, so vast, so overwhelming, I agree. Let me help you break it down. Even if you've never paused long enough to really think through what you want from your life, and the relationships in your life, it's in you. I want to help you with an exercise that will help you bring this to the front for you to look at, decide whether it's really what you want, and actively choose to put it on your list. And I'm not talking about vague ideas; you'll want to get as specific as possible.

"I want to be happy" sounds nice, but what does that really mean? In my life I've found that many things that I thought would make me happy actually didn't provide the desired happiness. Even if you can attain a given thing or outcome, it may feel good for a while, but what makes you happy changes with circumstances. Happiness is a feeling. It's fleeting. Instead, you might say, "I want to practice not being so controlled by my emotions." Now, that's something you can work toward! If happiness is dependent on things happening to you or for you, then it takes away your power. Joy, however, is what comes in spite of your circumstances. Joy is settled inwardly.

When you choose to work on goals that are attainable and measurable, you get a win. We all need to get a win under our belts. When we do, we feel empowered to take on bigger areas where we'd like to see healthier interaction.

I have to believe most people desire to have a healthy marriage and close, healthy family relationships. No one stands at the altar or before a judge and wants it to end badly. So what happens between that glorious, hope-filled moment captured in the photo—when the bride and groom are smiling after having just been pronounced man and wife—and the ugly, painful separation of divorce? How does it go so wrong, so many times, both inside and outside the church? Well, there are lots of intricate reasons for this in each unique relationship, but somewhere along the line, expectations don't meet reality, and communication stops being healthy—or stops altogether—and that breathing, living oneness of marriage suddenly starts to die as the two take back their singleness with both small and large choices.

While I have never been through a divorce myself, I have walked that painful path with loved ones, and it is a death. For some, it's even worse than death, because somewhere along the way, one or both chose to pursue a different life story—without the other. Again, I'm not talking about abuse or unsafe relationships; I'm talking about the multitude of divorces that occur because beautiful love stories get off track. The truth is, every relationship is at risk. We make daily choices that support—or are in conflict with—the marriage that we, at one point, chose. We get to choose to stay and work on the health of the marriage . . . or not. Both have consequences: one is life and growth, and the other is the slow fade to death of the marriage. We get to choose.

While most people might say, "Of course, I choose to make my marriage work," for many of us, whether we're age twenty or age sixty, we just don't have a clue what it takes to connect the desire for a fulfilling marriage to the behaviors that create one. So, what do we do? We might look to movies or TV or romance novels to help us set our expectations for marriage and family. Unrealistic expectations. If the only healthy relationships you know of come from TV or movies, or even from looking in on a family or marriage on social media, I can assure you that your expectations won't meet your reality.

KC desired deeply to be married. From the time he was eighteen till the time I reconnected with him at age twenty-nine, KC will openly tell you he tried to marry every girl he dated. I'm not saying that sarcastically: it's actually true. He was engaged a couple of times, and married and divorced once by the time I met him. He says, "I knew that I wanted that happy family and marriage, I just had no clue how to create it because I'd never seen it."

When I began to date my man he was definitely a diamond in the rough—emphasis on "in the rough." Honestly, we both were. One of the many things that drew me to KC was something I highly respected. He had an open mind and a willing heart to learn what went contrary to everything he'd seen and tried. The reason he was so teachable is because his purpose was what drove him. At the core of who he was, KC knew that he wanted a marriage different from what he had experienced growing up, and though he already had a painful failed attempt in his first marriage, he was all the more resolved to make it right in ours. We know firsthand that it takes years to undo old, unhealthy ways of doing things. And it takes patience and perseverance on the part of both of us to struggle through the hard, and sometimes painful, steps toward learning something completely counterintuitive.

KC and I were no different from anyone else when we married. We were in love, we wanted to grow old together, and we wanted to have a family. Beyond that, we had hopes to own a home, maybe have a dog, and take fun family vacations together. We had what Simon Sinek calls a big WHY. If you've never read Simon's book *Find Your Why*, I recommend it. It's for leaders (spouses are leaders, of themselves and of a home), and it's for people building a tribe (a family is a tribe), and it's to help you find the foundational purpose that drives you to daily move in the direction of fulfilling that purpose with passion and undeterred focus. The book doesn't differentiate between a business owner's WHY and an individual's WHY, but in the book, Simon says this:

> Each of us has one WHY. It's not a statement about who we aspire to be; it expresses who we are when we are at our natural best. If you're already unconsciously living your WHY, then spelling it out for yourself will turn it into an even more powerful tool. And if you're struggling to live your WHY, then finally understanding your purpose, cause, or belief can help you change course and realign with a new perspective . . . to help you find the feeling of fulfillment that may have eluded you thus far.[7]

Knowing who you are at your natural best and bringing that into your marriage becomes a powerful tool for shaping each of you within the boundaries of a marriage. Rather than unconsciously winging it from day to day, the better you understand yourself, the more apt you are to choose to show up as your best self for stronger, clearer conversations with your spouse. We go through a whole session with couples before the wedding where we have them each answer 100 questions about what they believe about marriage and what it might look like once they are married. The SYMBIS (Saving Your Marriage Before It Starts) Assessment asks what the bride or groom wants out of marriage, what expectations they have about a broad range of things that are common in marriage, and how they plan to interact with all the other relationships in their lives: relationships like his parents and siblings, her parents and siblings, their single friends, the couple's social calendar, and church involvement, to name a few. The assessment gets couples talking about houschold jobs that arc commonly divided up, such as creating a budget, paying bills, grocery shopping, cooking, laundry, car maintenance, and yard work. Of course, you can't know how it actually plays out until you are living in the same space and married, but it's a great exercise to address the realities of marriage before you are married! When we learn how to define and live our purpose with focus and intentionality in each aspect of our lives, merge our purpose with another human, and address our expectations, great conversations are opened and areas where you may differ are revealed.

If you know what you really want your marriage to be, and you are partnered with someone who is resolved to choose the harder path of healthy growth instead of knee-jerk reactive living, that's a marriage on a path to health. This a good place to mention what is obvious: one person cannot choose for the other. This one marriage requires both people to be engaged and actively trying. In real life, one might carry the bulk of the load for a season, but overall, both people need to be active in keeping the marriage alive and on a healthy path. You may be like us; I saw what a healthy marriage looked like, so I could show what I knew could work. Or, you both might be desiring to create something neither of you have ever seen up close and personal. That's why you're here. That's why I'm sharing what I've seen and experienced. No matter what you hear or read about healthy and fulfilling monogamy for life being a "thing of the past," or even unnatural, I want to encourage you from personal experience that marriage is, in fact, very relevant, achievable, and wonderful. And it's possible for you, if you desire it and are willing to do the hard work to make it happen—you can change the trends of broken, unsatisfying relationships in your family lineage.

I grew up watching TV families like the Bradys on *The Brady Bunch* and the Seavers on *Growing Pains*. My young adult kids watched the Camdens on *7th Heaven*. These TV families had between thirty and sixty minutes to solve a problem, teach a lesson or moral, and then tie a little bow at the "happily ever after" ending. These families were designed for entertainment value and shaping social opinion. A team of writers pieced together the perfect outcome excluding many, if not most, of the realities that happen in the process of real life. What this did was give hope to people who didn't have real-life examples but were looking for a family that made it work. However, along with that hope for something more came unrealistic expectations. In real life, problems don't resolve themselves in thirty to sixty minutes. Real-life problems are messy and complicated, and they take time to resolve, often through clunky emotion-filled conversation as we muddle through to a healthy resolution. We need practical tools, not just for addressing and resolving problems, but also for the real-life parts that are just messy. That's not typically shown in movies or on TV; and if it is, a TV mess somehow still seems decorative, like a prop.

But TV show or Facebook story, a snapshot does not a life make. Media representation can never tell the full story. You may see dozens of Instagram photos of your friend's fabulous vacation with their beloved, full of smiling faces and adventure. But no one posts about the piles of dirty clothes, the trash that needs to be taken out, the clogged toilet, the stack of papers to go through that clutter the counter, the late bill back at home, or the spot where the dog peed on the carpet for the tenth time. While normal, no one wants to see the little grumpy moments and bickering about scheduling or whose turn it is to pick up the kids or do the dishes. Scratch beneath the surface of those little moments, and you find the bigger things, like deciding whose family to spend the holidays with or how to parent in different situations that come up as our kids grow up—things we don't feel adequately prepared for. Those moments happen every day, yet you will never see them on a Facebook status; or, when you do, it might be an awkward moment when someone went on a rant and left us feeling like that was a little *too real* for social media.

Even reality families on TV don't show the full picture. Arguably the most famous reality family, the Kardashians, shared many private moments in front the of the camera for twenty seasons. While we've seen a bit more of their process, even their reality is a highly edited version. Yes, the Kardashians are an actual family, and yes, they show more bumps in the road than the average family does on social media, but there are still many difficult conversations and moments that happen outside of the camera, as they should. We may think we have the whole picture of the Kardashians, the most public family today, but we are mistaken. We don't have even close to the whole picture. And yet, their global audience believes they know them inside and out. The truth is that they are brilliant marketers of a lifestory people want to watch. They edit an entire week down to a thirty-minute show.

I think it's important to put something out there to show *how* a healthy and realistic marriage plays out alongside, or smack in the middle of, the messy. As a young bride, I wanted a book that adequately equipped me, met me where I was, and helped me get to who and where I wanted to be in my marriage in a realistic way. Many stories, especially in faith-based books, can tend to come off as neat and tidy, with men and women who choose the right, hard thing every time. Maybe our marriage was more clunky in our communication than most, because we messed up a lot in the process. Those were the areas I needed help navigating. It's why I share the many lame attempts that KC and I made at healthy communication: to show you that it doesn't always flow well. I find it comforting to know that all couples have embarrassing moments we'd rather no one knew about. It's also comforting to have hope that we can learn to grow through them, together. You and your person will choose what you want for your marriage, and I'm telling you now that it will be normal to fumble through the process. By sharing our sometimes immature moments, my hope is to let you see that you're by far not the only one who feels like it's possibly getting worse before it gets better.

I remember reading leadership books by John Maxwell in my twenties and thirties and implementing the principles in my marriage and eventually our family. While the language and particulars of running a business compared to running a family are definitely different (one can't necessarily fire their spouse when they don't maintain family culture), I felt like the principles found in John's books were my saving grace because of their heavy focus on integrity in our relationships and culture. When John wrote about creating a culture in a business setting, I saw how to create what I wanted for my marriage and family. When he taught about problem-solving on a team, I applied those problem-solving skills in my marriage and with my children. Interestingly, in these leadership books, I found practical steps that I could immediately put into play to lead myself as I navigated through times when our communication was productive and when our communication didn't flow. Lots of books talk about marriage being for life, but I wanted practical steps, so we could make that happen. Tools that work for folks like you and me who are building a marriage we've only heard of, dreamt of, or hoped for. No longer do we need to settle for less than what we desire because we don't know how to connect where we are to what we want.

KC and I have mentored people who have either fallen into a rut or stopped dreaming of an ideal for one of two reasons: one, they didn't have a plan or two, hardship hit, and they went into survival mode. When you and your spouse disagree and don't handle it well, communication afterward can become dysfunctional or nonexistent. For some, this pattern goes on for enough time that there is a tipping point when held resentment or an emotional flatline becomes the elephant in the room. For others, there is pain that comes from boredom ("this is all there is?") or from mishandled circumstances compounded over time. Many of us take life as it happens to us and don't stop to challenge it. To choose something different than what we have. To stop and really choose the life we want for ourselves and our marriage. Together. By the time a couple reaches out for marriage mentoring of any kind, whether in person or by picking up a book like this one, they are often frustrated and feel angry or numb or a variety of emotions stemming from unmet expectations.

One of the first things KC likes to ask a couple in mentoring, and what I'll ask you now, is, "Do you want this marriage to work? Is this marriage worth saving to you?" Belief informs behavior. If a couple believes their marriage can last for life, or be salvaged, even if they don't know how in that moment, it shows that they will be willing to work on the steps to see it through. This is why the question is so pertinent to moving forward. In order for us to change our behavior, we need to believe the marriage is worth the work. We need to want it. Then, the issue becomes a matter of "will you?" and "how?"

Our marriage and family can be the legacy that we leave to the next generation. John Maxwell says it this way: "There is value in considering what you want your life to stand for. Only by changing the way you live will you be able to create the legacy you want to leave." We're here to help you create your legacy. And how you create a legacy is through choices, and daily, consistent behaviors to support those choices.

One day over coffee, a dear friend said to me, in an honest, vulnerable moment, "I asked a friend who has been married for more than thirty years what her secret was to both staying married and being in love for life, and she said, 'I've chosen to marry him many times over the years in my heart.' Wow," said my friend, "that moved me. I love my husband that I'm married to today, but I can't help but wonder what my life might look like now if someone had spoken that into my life when I was married to my first husband." It's simple, yet profound: staying married for life is not a one-time decision in a ceremony, but rather, years of daily decisions recommitting to the original promise.

> Staying married for life is not a one-time decision in a ceremony, but rather, years of daily decisions recommitting to the original promise.

Most of us stand at the altar vowing to stay married for better and for worse, till death do us part, but don't plan for our marriage as much as we plan for our wedding. And sometimes it takes a wake-up call to show us what's really at stake. For me, it came in the form of a dream.

Years ago, when our four oldest kids were little and before the younger two were born, things between KC and me were good, but sort of ho-hum. We had fallen into the rut of raising kids and living busy lives. Nothing was particularly wrong, we just needed to pay a bit more attention to our relationship to avoid growing apart.

One night during that time, I woke up with my heart racing from a nightmare. In the dream, I had cheated on KC. The dream started at that place—me with the knowledge of having cheated with some nameless, faceless person. You know how dreams aren't always linear, and don't always make sense? This one was very real. In this dream, I was walking from my car up to my front door, when the realization hit me. Dread and regret gripped me. *What have I done?* I thought in my dream as I walked through the front door of my home, where KC and the kids were waiting. I came through the door with the knowledge of having just cheated, while they all thought I'd been away on a business trip. KC and our two oldest kids were doing the after-dinner dishes, and the younger two were watching TV in the living room. "Mooom!" they yelled for me just as they did in real life when I actually came home from work travel. As soon as they saw me, they were jumping over couches and coffee table to get to me. KC smiled sweetly from the sink and said, "Hi, babe! Welcome home!"

The dread I felt in that dream was like a kick to the stomach, and it brought me abruptly awake. I sat up with a start. KC was peacefully sleeping beside me, and I cannot tell you the relief I felt as I lay back down, reminding myself over and over, "It was only a dream. It was only a dream." I started to cry at what a terrible feeling it was to have done something so irreversible. I could not erase from my mind what it felt like to have done something that was 100 percent in my power to have avoided. I remember praying, thanking God and committing to myself to never forget that feeling. Nothing would ever be worth that feeling. What I wanted in the long term can never be, will never be, fulfilled if I let down my internal boundary to expose myself to a potential threat to my marriage: a romantic, emotional, or physical intimate connection to someone other than KC. That's a clear boundary for me. As I shared that dream with my husband the next day, I said that I wanted us to be more intentional about keeping our relationship alive and growing, and never getting lazy in our interaction.

The situation that was my nightmare is commonly found in romance novels or seen in movies or on TV shows when people don't have boundaries and safeguards up around their marriages. Maybe they are in a fight or a season when they are struggling to connect, and it's putting strain on the relationship. The story sets us up as the audience to root for the infidelity that is sure to present itself—a character in a weakened state meets someone they have chemistry with, and because we've just seen how they struggle to be seen, understood, or appreciated in their marriage relationship, we are led right into rooting for them to give in to their passion. I am sorry to say that as a younger person, I have gotten swept up into the plot, reading or watching to see the story build to the moment when they give in to it. What the story might not show is the scenario I lived in my dream: walking through the front door to a family that doesn't know about the infidelity, looking into the eyes of the person they made a promise to, and seeing the children they are raising together. We don't see the character when regret sets in as they have those first few conversations with their family after the irreversible has been done. Why don't the movies show that? Because it's not only unsexy, it's sad. It's a death to a promise, and who wants to pay to read or watch that? That's no longer entertainment. It's no dream. It's all too real for too many.

If you have lived this situation in reality, I want you to hear that there is no judgment from me, only love. Whatever your past, I want you to have the life you truly want for yourself in the long game from this point forward. I know that sometimes it takes a real friend to speak the hard truth even if it might hurt. When we are honest with one another—not blandly politically correct or encouraging each other to live for personal happiness no matter the cost to others—but when we speak to one another on a real level, we can stretch and grow and face some hard truths. Marriage for life includes some hard truths, and staying married for life will come at a cost, like it does for every single person who commits to being married for life. That cost is not bad. It's buy-in. It's your skin in the game to keep coming back.

Anything worth having has uphill moments, and in order to have something you desire (a strong, lasting marriage), it will cost some things in the process. But what an investment! If you've had that conversation, both with yourself and your spouse, and if you've resolved in your minds that what you're working for is far bigger than momentary comfort or temporary self-serving happiness, you're taking intentional steps toward your heart's deepest desire.

If you happen to be in a rut in your relationship, let my bad dream wake you up too. The pain of regret is far stronger than any momentary happiness that misplaced, impulsive passion can bring. If you are caught in the tension of having chemistry with another person, or dream of chemistry with someone other than your spouse, let me throw some cold water on you. Eventually, if you give in to that passion and enter into a relationship with another person, they're human too. You *will* have conflict or get to the same place of impasse with that person too. When we don't work past or through the sticking point in one relationship but quit and move on instead, we never grow beyond that spot that inevitably comes in every relationship. We can create a whole lot of wreckage in the process of pursuing a connection with someone other than our spouse. If you intentionally continue to choose your spouse for life, your emotions and passions can be revived again and again and again over the course of a lifetime.

> When we don't work past or through the sticking point in one relationship but quit and move on, we never grow beyond that spot that inevitably comes in every relationship.

I have a friend who has been married three times. Her first two marriages lasted about three or four years. She will jokingly admit that communication is not her strong suit. When her third marriage came to that four-year mark, things were again under pressure.

Rather than quit and move on to the next relationship, as she had in the past, she did something she hadn't done before; she chose to stay. She worked on developing her communication skills. I won't say its been smooth sailing for her, because it's never smooth sailing for anyone trying to grow past a personal limit, but today, she is still married after ten years. She says she learned that every time she got to a certain pressure point in her prior relationships, she walked away, believing she'd either grown apart from her previous husbands or that they just weren't a match anymore. But what she realized after two painful divorces, and with a third marriage hanging in the balance, was that the root issue that was the undoing of her first two marriages was not gone when they divorced and she found a new person to love. She carried it right with her into the next marriage. *She* did. It was only when she chose to not have a third divorce and get to work on her communication skills that she was able to grow past the point that led to the end of her previous marriages. It wasn't until she got real with herself and looked at the common denominator—herself—in all of her marriages, that she got to work on changing the future of her marriage. What a beautiful internal pivot!

I love this quote from the great wizard Dumbledore from the *Harry Potter* books: "There will be a time when we must choose between what is right and what is easy."[8] Actually, there are many opportunities for us to make that choice. And only you get to make the decision for yourself.

Cast Your Vision

Let's look at some realistic examples of what you might choose for what you want for your marriage and family relationships. I call this casting your vision. In order to do this, you'll need to schedule some regular time on your calendar when you will give focus and energy to work on yourself. Growth is a big piece of changing the trajectory of your life and marriage. This is not about putting Band-Aids on symptoms with quick fixes, or putting all of your attention on the issue of the day; it's about getting to the root of your role in the marriage and your expectations as you analyze your relationship, and then doing something with what you learn. It can be a big, overarching decision that helps you steer your relationship, or something smaller that helps you navigate day-to-day issues that pop up. To get your creative juices flowing, here are some things you might connect with. Feel free to mark or copy the ones that reflect your goals, and add your own.

- I choose to do the work to become the best version of myself.
- I choose to stop drinking, or lose weight, or get counseling for an unhealthy habit that is hindering my growth and relationship.
- I choose healthy communication habits.
- I choose healthy conflict resolution in my marriage and family.
- I choose to forgive more intentionally, or to forgive something in particular that I've been holding.
- I choose to set some boundaries around our marriage.
- I choose to move forward, trusting that both of us want a healthy marriage.
- I choose to have regular times when I talk with my spouse.
- I choose to believe the best of my spouse.
- I choose to stop making assumptions without asking clarifying questions.
- I choose to be a safe place for my spouse to process what's happening in his/her life.
- I choose to have more fun with my spouse.

Your list can be long; go big. Why not? It's your legacy you're talking about.

Healthily functioning marriages and families have a common trait. That trait is not perfect people or the rare, perfectly paired couple, but healthy and accurate communication. That just happens to be the second C, but it's also the underlying theme of this whole book. Connecting regularly through healthy communication is crucial to a thriving marriage for life.

Getting Rid of Your "Rock Pile"

Once you've made a list of choices that you'd like to focus on your marriage, look at some of your personal habits or behavioral patterns that might hinder those choices. Not your spouse's, yours. Identifying and taking responsibility for your part in perpetuating old unhealthy ways of interacting will make your spouse more apt to do the same. There is nothing that compares to a spouse humbly taking ownership for their part in making the relationship better! It opens your heart and unlocks your own willingness to look at your role in moving forward together with your person. Grab your notebook and pen or your tablet and go to your thinking place. Write down your thoughts as you process the areas in which you'd like to see healthy growth in your marriage, and the areas you want to personally improve upon to make that happen. This will be for your eyes only. Begin this step with a mindset that you're willing to release little things and be solution-focused. The goal is not to nurture anger by drudging up every unresolved situation for the last however many months or years. This is a time to look for patterns that are not being resolved in a way that leaves you both feeling like the matter is settled.

Next, if you are able, separate out the emotional response to each situation from the root of the issue in order to move forward with the conflict resolved. Ask yourself, *Is this a serious enough problem to address?* or *Is there a common theme to the little arguments that keep popping up?* Don't focus on the individual situation, but rather, focus on the root. This may be a bit confusing, so let me tell you a story to show you what I mean.

When KC and I were first married, we were given a Nintendo game system. At first, it was so fun after work to eat dinner and play a few games together. I had been a teenager in the Atari generation, and KC was of the Pong generation (Google it), which means we were both alive when home video games were invented and became mainstream. In 1990, having a Nintendo system felt so modern! Anyway, after a few weeks of trying to get my little Mario character to eat all the coins before I was killed, I got bored. It wasn't really fun to me anymore. KC, however, was into it, trying to see how many levels he could improve each time he cued up the game. We'd come home from work, and he'd play . . . alone. He'd hoot and holler when he was winning, wanting me to high five him for his success, and get irritated and frustrated when he'd make it farther in the game only to have his little character lose.

I assumed he'd notice I wasn't really into it and was starting to feel ignored. I began to make passive aggressive comments as I'd walk by him playing and he'd be so wrapped up in the game, I don't even know if he heard me. I'd do my nighttime routine, then read in my room (or seethe, probably both) till he stopped playing and would come looking for me to hang out. I'd freeze him out. He'd ask me what was wrong. "Nothing," I'd say, with my voice as flat and emotionless as I could muster to send him my underlying real meaning. He took me at face value and just let me be.

I built an entire case against him in my head over the course of a couple of days; each day building what my mom calls a "rock pile." My mom taught us the rock pile analogy when we were growing up. When you don't resolve an issue, you add it to your rock pile—a little (or big!) rock in an imaginary pile of other unresolved issues. Then, when the next argument or issue comes out, you pick up those rocks and pelt the other person with them, like verbal ammunition. If you've experienced this, you know exactly what I'm talking about, and you also probably know it's not good. You and I are not the only ones who do this, but trust me; it's not right or healthy. Put enough rocks in your pile, and you've eventually built a wall that separates you from your spouse, a fortification for an ongoing war. You can injure your beloved—and relationship—sometimes beyond repair. It's the dead opposite effect of what you want to accomplish.

When I finally confronted KC over the Nintendo system issue, I was furious. I started throwing verbal "rocks" at him. It's been so many years ago that I can't honestly tell you today *what* I said, but I know that I blasted him. We had just come home from work, and I was ready to tell it to him straight. Honestly, in hindsight, I don't know what I expected him to do. Deep down, what did I really want? Whatever it might have been, my method for getting there was all wrong. That poor man got all of my worst fears, emotions, guilt-tripping and anger in one big emotional explosion he did not see coming. Over a video game.

But remember KC's family method of operation in conflict? This is what he saw growing up! Feeling backed into a corner, he engaged for battle. He responded angrily, equally as emotionally irrational. Then he just shut down, because when KC got mad, he couldn't think straight; he'd go into emotional lockdown. It was a disastrous fail on both of our parts. Not one outcome of the conversation was beneficial or on-topic. In the end, he was left reeling, and I still felt lonely. He didn't understand what the heck had just happened, and I felt hurt that he got mad when I was certain that *he knew* what he'd done had hurt me. Boy, did we blow that one. And it was not the only time, I'm sorry to say. But Nintendo wasn't the root. The root was learning to navigate communication about our expectations of how we spent our evenings together.

Those first few years were full of us trying to figure healthy communication out. Slowly but surely, we learned that both passive aggressive and aggressive responses are damaging and confusing. KC much prefers raw honesty, spoken clearly and right away, without too much emotion, and with respect. Who wouldn't prefer that to an ambush?

I also learned to speak long before I'm angry or I've built an imaginary case against my husband. That does no one any good. I also learned to not have expectations without a conversation ahead of time about those expectations. It helps us draw healthy boundaries. I can't get mad at KC for not meeting an expectation I have that I have never discussed with him, nor had buy-in from him on.

I'd made an assumption—a whole bunch of them—based on what I believed to be obvious, which also included unwritten, unagreed-upon "rules" of being married that I had in my head. Today, in the same scenario, I would be more apt to say, "Babe, can I talk to you about something, with your full attention?"

He would then have the option to say, "Yes, but can we do this later? I'm on my last player." We would then decide on an agreed-upon time to talk, like in ten minutes, or twenty. We would have then made the agreement, and we had already chosen that we wanted to honor our word to one another.

> **Listening and hearing are not the same thing.**

Alternatively, KC might be at a good breaking point in the game, turn from the screen, set down his controller to give me his full attention and say, "Sure, now's good. What's up?"

Whether we had agreed to talk later or in the moment, the stage would have been set: I have something to say, and I have said so before anger has taken hold, so when I bring it up, KC doesn't feel defensive. For his part, KC has acknowledged that he is making time to not just listen but to *hear* me. Did you get that? Listening and hearing are not the same thing. One is listening to the person talk but not really absorbing the information (or the emotion behind it) with a mindset to learn something about the other person. The other is creating the willingness and the mind space to really hear what the other is saying, and in doing so, seeking to understand and resolve what needs to be resolved. Huge difference, though hearing can be mimicked by a listening posture. The difference is in the listener choosing to just "do time" while the other person vents or blasts them, versus the hearer, who intentionally connects to the message the other is trying to convey for the sake of love, respect, and resolution.

To continue this hypothetical conversation the wiser version of me might have had, once KC gave me his attention, I might say, "I know we bought that game system to play together, but I'm bored with it now. I'm sorry if that disappoints you. I'm not saying I don't ever want to play, but at night after work, I'd rather come home and do something *with* you. I know you still like to play, so can we please set up some time boundaries when you can play, and from here on out, after work, can we make the focus about time doing something together that we both enjoy?"

Over the years, and through lots of of trial, error, and not giving up, I've learned to ask directly and succinctly for what I want without projecting the responsibility of my emotional response on KC. He has learned to hear what I'm really saying—or when the emotion still eclipses the message, he's learned to ask deeper questions to draw the message up to the surface. In that silly blow-up, nearly three decades ago, we both ended up apologizing, and he heard that I just wanted time with him. That was the root. I learned that he wasn't intending to ignore me—he just got caught up in the fun and competition of the game and didn't see that the old routine no longer worked for me. Two young, self-centered people with our own agendas, we figured out a way to come to an agreement that satisfied both of us. Neither of us were wrong in what we wanted, but we figured out how to say it in a nonthreatening way. And most importantly, we didn't bring up the Nintendo issue as ammunition in a future argument. We committed early on not to build a rock pile of resentment against one another, in order to make every effort to fight fair. To keep the issue at hand the issue at hand, and to keep a clean slate between us. Once we'd really truly resolved it, with apologies and forgiveness, we CHOSE our outcome: our relationship over anything else, even video games.

It took me a long time to understand that KC doesn't want to have to try picking up on my subtleties. He's not very good at it, and truthfully, I'm neither great at signaling or picking up on KC's own subtleties. KC would rather I approach him with loving, respectful, accurate communication to resolve things far before it turns into an out-and-out battle that hurts both of us and solves nothing. I had to learn to not count on his intuitively understanding what I want or need when I don't tell him. That's neither fair nor realistic. Have the courage to ask for what you want in a respectful, disarming manner. Vulnerable honesty is always the way to go.

Getting back to our exercise, with your end goal in mind, write out the areas where you'd like to see growth or where you'd like to work on being intentional about certain parts of your relationship. You can write out paragraphs or bullet points, however your mind processes, but be specific. If your communication has been poor until now, you may have built up a rock pile of your own, so at first it may get uglier before it gets better. You'll need to discern what things up to this point have been stored and perhaps even fueled with anger and hurt without being properly dealt with. The goal is for this to eventually become a cleansing, fresh-start activity. Study your relationship patterns. Do you see themes in your points of conflict rather than the individual situations? Look specifically for what you can take ownership of so this doesn't become an exercise in pointing fingers.

Remember, you don't want to build a wall out of your rock pile . . . the goal is to build a bridge. A bridge of healthy communication that connects you to your person when you stand separated by an issue.

Write it all out. Get it off your chest. It may feel very cathartic to do this. Venting every angry, pent-up negative thought to the person is not the way to begin a healthy path of communication, as you learned from my little Nintendo tantrum. Writing it out will be an exercise for you to unload and release the emotion attached to the situations to move forward in healing with a clear mind and positive tone. (Eventually the goal is to not need this because you'll be clearing the air on a regular basis.)

When you've written it all out, burn (or delete) your rantings. I once heard from a marriage and family therapist who advised that while it's good to journal and get things off your chest if you are prone to express yourself in writing, be sure to destroy your written rantings. God forbid something should happen to you and your loved ones find your temporary "mad rantings" but not have the opportunity to process them with you. I would never want my loved ones to find my ugliest vents in temporary private anger flare-ups and take them as my true or final feelings. Without me to explain that it's simply a brain-cleansing activity, they might be left with some terrible thoughts or inaccurate beliefs. So write and vent if you must, but shred, delete, or burn it immediately, or someone you love dearly could get burned by your words.

No One is Compatible

Some people need to talk to process. This is me. I no longer keep a rock pile built up, but as things happen, talking is part of my processing through it. I am very choosy as to who I process with, and I advise you to be the same, if you're a talking processor. If you're just starting out, and have quite a few things to process through, I can tell you it might be a wise decision to process with a therapist. There have been times when I knew that in order to move forward, I needed to get unblocked, and at times, I did so with a trusted and highly recommended therapist who shares my core beliefs, isn't emotionally attached to my problems, and is focused on helping me find the path to resolution. I went to someone I trusted and asked for a referral to a licensed therapist who shares my faith. The goal is to get someone who can give you tools to work on yourself to get unstuck. I have done this for myself and my kids, and I have advised the people I love and mentor to do the same. Sometimes we are just too close to a situation to see clearly, and a healthy, trained eye can help us identify the root and walk us through.

Remember, not all input is equal. We have to guard our relationship from wrong, though well-meaning, advice. Once, at a time when KC and I were in a season of rocky communication, I had a dear, well-meaning friend give me terrible advice with the best of intentions. She saw that I was troubled. She wanted to help. She advised me to consider if the marriage was still working for me, since I didn't appear to be very happy. "Life is too short to not be happy," she said. This precious friend was doing her best to encourage me and was deeply sincere. But, as mentioned previously, a person can be sincere and sincerely wrong at the same time. We must discern whom we allow to speak into our most cherished relationships. In our discerning, we must also choose whether we will emotionally climb on an escape train, or put up a boundary and choose to stay because we know that what we're working for is more important than quitting in a temporary, unhappy season. Emotional support that guides you away from what you ultimately want, though delivered with loving intentions, is dangerous when we are vulnerable. I remember saying to my friend, "I appreciate you loving me and wanting the best for me, but everything I want for the long-term *includes* KC."

A few years ago, we attended a lovely outdoor wedding up on a cliffside overlooking the California coast in Santa Barbara. It was the golden hour when the bride and her dad walked down the aisle and he put her hand in her groom's hand. Here these sweet young adults were, making a promise to one another and a covenant with God, with their whole lives out in front of them. KC and I love weddings. We love love. I find it so romantic to hear both the traditional, timeless vows that generations before have promised, as well as the unique, more modern version of vows that couples have written for one another as they profess their love and loyalty to each other for as long as they both shall live. KC and I always sit a little closer and hold hands a little tighter after weddings because it reminds us of our own vows and the covenant that we made. All these years later, the power of the million little re-commitments we make to one another in hard times and good has only magnified the original promise.

This wedding was particularly special because the couple were close friends of our eldest daughter Holli and her then-new-husband James. They'd all met in college, and we'd grown to love them over the years through visiting the campus or having them come stay in our home. Katie and John Detrich, the bride and groom, had both stood beside Holli and James just a few months before as our daughter and son-in-law spoke their vows to one another, and now it was their turn. It was so meaningful for us to watch this young couple make their promises, and to look at Holli and James—both in the wedding party—looking sweetly at one another, their faces showing that they were remembering their own vows. That was my brain during the wedding; jumping back and forth between what the pastor was saying, thinking of how far our journey had taken us since our own vows, and reading Holli and James' faces as they did the same. Round and round my attention went. It was almost too much love to take in, so my brain was pinging all over.

As I tuned back in to the pastor, it was just in time to hear something I'd not heard at a wedding before. He said, "I have had the privilege of doing pre-marital mentoring with Katie and John. There's something I haven't told you before but will tell you now. Some of you might be thinking, *Oh, John and Katie are so perfectly compatible!* But I want to tell you that I have found them *not* to be compatible." He paused for dramatic effect. It worked. Everyone was awkwardly quiet as they waited for him to explain. "Because . . . no one is compatible. Every couple that gets married is made up of two imperfect, flawed people who have chosen to become compatible. And that, my friends, takes a lifetime of growing together." That's good, isn't it? It completely blows the idea out of the water that some couples are compatible and others aren't. True, some personalities have less conflict, but becoming compatible takes a lifetime of process, not to mention a fair share of different kinds of trials that require effort to work through together. Compatibility is both people choosing to work toward a common end picture they have in mind, which is all about time and intentionally growing through your lifetime together.

Imagine Your Future

I want to share another thinking exercise I do often, and it's a fun one. This is something I do to ensure I'm living intentionally and creating the life I truly want to live as much as it depends on me. I'd like to invite you to give it a try. Go to your thinking space and sit down with a pen and notebook or your tablet (I use both). Now . . . allow yourself to imagine. It's a beautiful word, and an even lovelier exercise. One we don't do enough of as adults. My adult kids were so good at using their imaginations every day when they were little, but as adults they don't do it nearly as much. We are like that too.

Imagine. Imagine what your life looks like as a 90-year-old you. Do you see it? Where are you sitting? Is anyone beside you? In my scenario I'm sitting on a porch as the sun goes down, rocking in a chair next to KC with a feeling of contentment, looking back on my life. You'll "look back" on your own life. What do you see?

- What does your relationship with your spouse look like?
- What does the relationship with your adult kids (if you had kids) look like?
- What was your family culture?
- What does your relationship with your grandkids look like?
- What kind of life did you live?
- What kind of friendships did you have?
- Did you travel?
- Where did you live?
- What did you accomplish in your business?
- Did you accomplish big things?
- Did you pay attention to the little details?
- Did you have a cause that you gave your life to?
- What do people closest to you say about you?
- What kind of experiences do you often revisit because they were so good or meaningful?
- What stories do you tell often?

Those are questions to get you started, but let your story look however you want it to. I firmly believe that it's important to look at how I want my life to look on the backside, rather than living day to day until my time is up. I am particular about how I want my life to play out; are you? There are things I want to accomplish, specific things I want to pour into my kids and grandkids, and that means there are decisions I need to make between now and that time to ensure I accomplish them, if I'm blessed to live that long. I can only imagine that you do too, or at least if you've never thought of it, I'm glad you're starting now. Again, referring to John Maxwell's way of putting it: "There is value in considering what you want your life to stand for. Only by changing the way you live will you be able to create the legacy you want to leave." Think about what you want your life to look like and to stand for. Maybe you've never thought about your legacy. This is a great exercise to begin that thought process. A legacy is quite different than an inheritance; an inheritance is what we leave *to* our loved ones, and a legacy is what we leave *in* them. Memories of us and the way we made them feel. Once you've established what you'd like your life to have looked like, come back to today and intentionally connect the dots between today and that day way off in the future that you just visited. To reengineer your life from today to *that* day, make choices that create the kind of life you desire to have lived, and then *go live it.*

> An inheritance is what we leave *to* our loved ones, and our legacy is what we leave *in* them.

I hope you're not feeling that it's impossible or unrealistic, your venturing into the ideal of how you want your life to look. Maybe you've had some hardships in life that have left you feeling out of control, and the idea of setting a plan in place, only to run the risk of perhaps losing something or someone dear leaves you feeling like, what's the point? Allow me to encourage you. Yes, things can happen that we won't expect, and hard things, sometimes devastatingly hard things that are out of our control. Those things are going to happen whether you are working toward something or not. Have you ever been hit with something completely out of your control? Something out of left field and painful and life altering? I have. But there is a big difference between having it hit when you are allowing life to move you from day to day, versus when you're living on purpose with a plan that you're working and growing toward. When a tragedy or heartache strikes it's far easier to recover and recalibrate when you have something you're working toward. Responding in healthy ways when the unexpected happens adds to our legacy.

As we focus on living intentionally and creating the life we choose rather than what is handed to us, we stop playing defense and move into an offensive position. Knowing what you want from life and having an ever-evolving plan on how to accomplish it will serve as a North Star as you navigate both the hard and wonderful things that happen to you.

Identifying what you want to accomplish in your life is the first step to identifying what really matters to you and what will propel you forward in your life. When you were a kid, did your parents give you a list of chores? When I was growing up, Saturday morning was chore time in our family. When we woke up, if we had anything we wanted to do that day, we had to finish the list of chores our mom had put on the kitchen table before we could go. On the days when I had plans with my friends, I was highly motivated to get all of my work done early, so I could get out of the house to my friends. Conversely, on the days when I had no plans and wanted to just laze around all day, I was flatlined in motivation to start—let alone finish—my chores. It's the same as an adult. If we have no plan of where we're going or what we want our life to count for, getting the boring, mundane, or hard stuff done is deflating (and we all have boring, mundane, and hard stuff.) We feel tired before we start. Lack of purpose and positive direction can keep us stagnant and even depressed for days, weeks, or even years. But having a goal clearly in sight will help to energize and motivate you to push through.

Positive Communication

As you work through the process of understanding, in positive language, what is important to you, you'll want to use that same positivity when sharing your vision with your spouse. I've found that *how* I package information that I care about matters when I share it with KC, and vice versa. I can tell you right now that if I state it bluntly and cut right to the chase without any lead in, he shuts down, or worse, gets defensive because he feels I'm being critical. I find it interesting that while I know I need to do this at work with my team, and am pretty good at lovingly and intentionally packaging what I'm saying to them, I am tempted to blurt out my thoughts with my husband, and in doing so, I come across as way too blunt. When I'm not being intentional, my words and tone of voice can come across as critical, which is the last thing I want to do! I want to share my heart, I want him to hear me, and ideally I would like us to work together toward the end goal.

If you've never taken the time to choose your words wisely and thoughtfully, you know exactly the outcome I'm describing: defensive, ears closed, and body language that says the other person has shut down before even getting into the conversation. That's why it's so important to take the time to figure out the "why" and "what" of what you're going to discuss with your spouse before you communicate it, which is what the next chapter is all about.

Action Steps

1. Arrange some time and a place to think and process. Set the appointment with yourself, block it out on your calendar, and keep the appointment. Remember to avoid all distractions—set your phone alarm if you have to so you don't check the time every three minutes, and put your phone on airplane mode.

2. Create an environment for this time that will be one you look forward to. It should be a space for thinking and writing that pleases your senses: a comfortable chair, a view that inspires

you to think (not a cluttered space that makes you want to get up and straighten things out), a scented candle, a quiet space, or sometimes background music that isn't distracting or a warm cup of tea or coffee to hold in a mug that means something to you. When you make time to be alone with your thoughts in an inviting place, you'll look forward to getting there each day.

3. Write out your thoughts about the things that matter to you in your relationship and do so with a positive mindset rather than negative. Your attitude matters when you are imagining change. Think back to all the things you love about your spouse. Remember why you married him/her. What did you start out dreaming for your marriage to look like or represent? Write whatever comes to mind, whether on a notepad that you love, with a favorite pen, or in your iPad or notebook. Start jotting down your thoughts. The goal is to capture and process your ideas and thoughts in a way that works for you, so don't get caught up in what the "right" way is to do it. Whether your notes are old school or high tech, the goal is to make sure it gets done.

4. Allow yourself time to imagine. Be thoughtful as you think of what you really want your life to look like at the end, and jot those ideas down. If ideas on how to implement them come up, jot those down too, and highlight them with a different color so you can find them easily when you flip back through. Concentrate on the what and the why. What do you want in your life, marriage, and family culture? Why is it important to you? Don't be afraid to go deep. And have fun! Go big! Life wasn't meant to be lived small.

Chapter 3

Communicate Clearly and Calmly

"Communication to a marriage
is like oxygen to life. Without it, it dies."[9]
—Tony Gaskins

Communication is the second C. It's at the heart of every relationship, and therefore of this entire five-step process. Author Peter Velander says, "Healthy and accurate communication is one of the key characteristics of a marriage functioning well."[10] This means it's also safe to say that when a marriage is struggling, a lack of, or poor communication is typically at the root of the issue. Communication is the area where so many married couples struggle and get stuck. The goal is not perfect communication, but finding a comfortable rhythm for how to go through the communication (and perhaps even more so: miscommunication) process. Let me assure you right now: you can improve your communication with your fiancé or spouse. I can say that because we've mentored countless couples who struggle in this area, and we've seen that when they are both committed to making their communication better, it gets better. It might be clunky and feel awkward the first several times of starting a new way of interacting with one another, but it will get better over time, as you stick with it.

Think of regular, healthy communication with your spouse as the protective shield that the two of you build around your marriage. When you regularly discuss things that aren't currently flowing well, the less apt you are to have gaps that can allow unresolved conflict or issues to divide you.

Gaps happen all the time as we grow and change into different versions of ourselves over the years. It's not the gaps that are the problem; gaps are a sign of development, a break in the flow of "the way it's been working." Gaps show a growth spurt, kind of like when you were back in puberty and put on your favorite pair of jeans, only to find them way too short. The gap between the end of your jeans and the top of your shoe shows that growth has happened, and the fit is different. You didn't even notice the change, perhaps. There's just an obvious visual sign that growth took place. That person wearing the jeans that no longer fit is still you, just a new version of you. You will continue to grow emotionally long past puberty, if you choose to do so. Long past the wedding day. Hopefully, we are lifelong learners and growers. It's not a given, but hopefully through the process of growing older, we lean into growth: mentally, emotionally, and spiritually. While it might not be as visual as your jeans, you may be feeling the effects of a gap in your marriage. The gap isn't the problem. The gap is to be expected. The problem builds when you don't communicate as soon as one of you starts to feel it, with the intention to quickly bridge the gap.

Look, change is going to happen, at many times, at different paces, and in different ways, but I'll tell it to you straight—healthy growth comes from change *only* if you choose to grow. Change is inevitable; growth is optional. It's all in whether you expect it, prepare for it and choose to engage moving forward.

> **Change is inevitable; growth is optional.**

I haven't met very many people who radically changed overnight; in fact, I can't think of one. I'm talking about core beliefs and opinions in how they think, how they process situations, what they think about things that are important to them, and how they feel about someone. I haven't known of anyone who woke up one day and completely changed the way they show and receive love, frustration, or concern. You might know someone who one day seemed totally different, maybe a friend or a spouse. The truth is that when that kind of change or distance has occurred, there was a lot of behind-the-scenes thinking and process-ing and non-communication going on before the change was obvious outwardly. Maybe along the way you asked, "Is everything alright?" or "Are you upset with me? You seem distant," and a less-than-truthful answer was given. "I'm fine." "Nope. All good." Except it wasn't. I'm not saying it was intentional; they may not have slowed down enough to self-assess. They may have just felt something, and in pushing it down and not addressing it, they actually were allowing it to grow. You've heard of those people who just "grew apart." The phrase could be partially true, but more likely, things were left uncommunicated, creating a separation between two people. Compounded things along the way began to eat away at the promise.

Emotional gaps can be caused by individual growth. When one of you experiences growth, it can create division. It's a common struggle that every married couple has to work through and must be on the lookout for. This is similar to weight loss. I can remember when a friend of mine from church suddenly looked really trim one Sunday. "Oh my gosh!" I said. "Have you lost weight?" "Yes!" he said, excited that I'd noticed. "Thanks for noticing. I've lost 40 pounds!" I was stunned. Beyond it being awkward, it was amazing that even while seeing my friend every Sunday, up to that point I hadn't noticed. Forty pounds doesn't just happen. He did a lot of consistent work to get that weight off. Work that had happened in private and suddenly showed up publicly.

The same kind of change can go on in one's mind. When we spend time thinking things but not discussing them, by the time that gap shows up outwardly, it can seem like a shock to the person we haven't been communicating with. That's why regular communication is vital to the health of a marriage. Regular communication prevents unhealthy thinking from taking on a life of its own in our minds.

Change can be perceived as good, bad, or neutral to you or your spouse. If we are intentionally choosing to pursue growth in our life, our thoughts will expand and shift on all sorts of topics. This could be as simple as becoming a tidier person to bring order to your home, or having your passion stoked by learning about a need in the community and wanting to be a part of the solution. Maybe you developed an interest in learning a new skill or want to take up a new hobby. Sometimes, outside change like a loss of a job or financial crisis can emotionally impact the way you and your spouse engage with one another. If a spouse becomes detached or hits an emotional slump or low, that can dramatically change the way you interact. In some cases it's a big shift, like a change in your belief about God and how you choose for that belief to influence the way you live your life, or one of you desiring to change careers or move somewhere new. Over a lifetime, the people you are when you get married change in both small and large ways, so using your communication tools keeps you on the same page, even as you might approach it differently.

KC and I have been married for over three decades, and while today we have a thriving, loving marriage, when we are annoyed with one another or can't seem to get on the same page on an issue, we still use these same tools I'm sharing with you. A lot of our problems in the beginning were because we weren't addressing the root cause, which was a communication problem; we each just thought the other person needed to be more . . . something! If I'm honest we both probably thought the other needed to be more like "me." How wonderful to find that neither of us needed to change to become like the other person, but instead grow to become the next best version of ourselves.

Much easier! And once we learned to pick up and use (key word here: use) communication tools, we found that they worked no matter the topic. I find it so encouraging that after all this time together, those tools continue to be our go-to for navigating our way through decisions and disagreements.

The truth is, whether you are seriously dating, engaged, or have been married for any amount of time, the same basic tools of communication apply across the board. The good news is you improve at it with experience. Having been married for so many years, we have gotten better and better at recognizing which tool is needed and using it more quickly and. Even still, communication can be clunky. Sometimes we find ourselves in the same ridiculous heated discussion for the umpteenth time, and I wonder, *Why are we still not settled on this?* I'll tell you why. Because we are two imperfect and differently wired people who are merging our lives for life, and it's hard work to refine yourself, let alone invite a partner in to be part of the process! The nice thing about doing the hard work to communicate healthily with your spouse is that there are both short and long-term rewards.

Open, honest, regular communication is an indicator of a healthy relationship. When you approach each disagreement or offense with the mindset to hear, be heard, and work to compromise and restore without tearing the other person or their ideas down, or allowing them to tear yours down, your communication becomes more and more effective. When you communicate with honesty and respect and keep no rocks in your pile (grudges or unresolved problems) you have more space to get back to enjoying one another.

Just like you did in puberty, you will both grow in spurts: emotionally and mentally. You'll have a season when you aren't bickering very much, and then other times it will seem like you can't agree on anything. Not even necessarily about big issues. I mean the little annoyances that feel far more irritating than you rationally know they should. Those are the times when you may be tempted to think you've grown in two different directions, or that you're not a fit like you used to be. No, that's absolutely part of going the distance with one person—it happens to all of us, and it matters how you mentally approach and view communication.

When I meet people who view communication as hard work, too much effort, or "the grind," rather than as an expected, challenging, normal part of merging two lives, it's probably because there is an unmet expectation. And when you have an unmet expectation based on the misconception that some marriages are meant to be and therefore work effortlessly, and some marriages just . . . don't, then it greatly affects your attitude and how you resolve conflicts in communication.

Most of us don't even realize our expectations of marriage. Based on the marriages we've seen in person, in movies, or #couplegoals on social media, we've all made assumptions about relationships and how they work based on what we've experienced and what other people allow us to see publicly. The truth is, in private, every couple has conflict; every couple has interactions with one another where both conscious and unconscious communication shape their relationship.

You might feel like you are the only one who has those feelings of annoyance at your spouse, but, rest assured, you are not the only one. Those annoyances are typically things that you either didn't notice before, or didn't notice how much they bugged you before you married. Because you felt so well matched before the wedding, you had the expectation that after the wedding it might be easier to overlook. Now you're finding it's driving you nuts.

You may be wondering how you didn't notice that he chewed loudly, left his dirty clothes on the floor, was so picky about being on time, or didn't floss his teeth faithfully. Or how did it escape your attention that she takes forever to get ready, dislikes video games so strongly, likes to keep a ridiculously tidy house, or runs her car on fumes without noticing she's nearly out of fuel? When we choose to merge our lives with another person, we naturally have unspoken expectations that seemingly are spotlighted after the wedding.

While it makes for a great movie, I think we've done a disservice to pass along that underlying "happily ever after" mindset. The truth is that marriage is perhaps the most challenging relationship to navigate, but one that develops you, grows you, and is deeply fulfilling—far more than any other human relationship.

That said, I do believe that some marriage matches are naturally easier to navigate than others. Some twosomes are more aligned in interests, beliefs, and temperament, but even people who view life through a very similar lens will have things they disagree on sharply. It's just the nature of humanity. That is why KC and I began offering marriage prep mentoring to other couples; the more you know what you're dealing with before you enter into marriage, the better your mindset as "the merge" begins. If you're married and thinking, *Oh no, we didn't know all of this ahead of time, maybe we shouldn't have gotten married*, let me encourage you that we didn't either! But we started using these tools as we learned about them, and things got easier because we both wanted our marriage to last.

In all of the marriages I have known that have gone the distance, I have found either two people who grunted it out and lasted, but barely, and not with a lot of joyful times; or two people who made it a priority to consistently connect in such a way that they grew closer together, two people who became lifelong partners seeking the "oneness" of marriage and experiencing much joy. Staying married for life isn't just about crossing life's finish line without killing each other, but making your relationship the best it could possibly be with another person, *your* person, and that takes a lifetime of fine-tuning our communication.

The interesting component is that all of these interactions are typically private, within the confidentiality of the home, and rightly so;

but it can be isolating as well. On one hand we want to keep our relationship protected from outside interference, but when we're struggling (and we all struggle) we tend to look outside at the picture other people have allowed to show publicly. We assume they've figured out something we haven't. That may or may not be true, but it's very easy to get caught in that comparison trap we explored earlier. This is especially true if you're only looking at social media, where people tend to show their life's highlight reel, or worse, beautifully staged moments. You may have an issue on your mind and then start scrolling through Instagram, comparing your situation to everything you see; or, you might even create new problems in your head and start to feel bitter and stuck. From there, the slippery slope is contradictory to the end result we've said we want: healthy, growing relationships.

Any growing relationship needs intentional communication in such a way that is healthy and productive. When we establish guidelines that fit what we desire for our life, it's much easier to refer back to what we may have strayed from when communication started to break down a little. Before we even talk to the other person, we need to do a little "pregaming." To clarify, I don't mean drinking before you are ready to communicate; on the contrary, I mean getting some things really clear and straight in your head and heart that will help the process of communication. The following are some areas in which you can get your mind right before you approach a conversation for change.

Talk to Yourself

The human I communicate most often with is myself. The human *you* communicate most with is yourself. You are the voice in your own head, listening to yourself. All. Day. Long. But if we are listening to ourselves all day every day, and allowing our behaviors to be navigated by our natural instincts without using discernment, can you see how that might not serve us well when we then communicate with the humans *outside* our head? In our heads we attach meanings and attitudes and intentions to what others say, and then we respond to them based on those assumptions and filters.

I confess that I have been guilty many times of attaching a meaning to KC's words based on what I heard in his tone and the way he worded a sentence. Maybe you do it too. I unconsciously hear it through my own filter and what I believe about a tone of voice, and it causes an emotional response in me. Then, without even meaning to, I say something to myself in my head about his intention, and bam! I've begun to build a case. It's a hard habit to break, and it requires an intentional extra step, or two, or three to stop an assumptive thought process before I've built an internal case against him. Instead, I practice pausing, taking inventory about how I'm feeling, what I'm responding to, and asking a few questions of him. Before I even involve him, I needed to get better at talking to myself. In that pause I might ask myself one or more of these questions: What words, look or tone triggered me? What possible belief about KC or our relationship did it reinforce in me? What is the emotion I am feeling (sad, hurt, angry, annoyed?) What do I need him to know? What do I need from him in order to move on, grudge-free, and for there to be a clean slate between us?

If we are not intentional in our communication with ourselves, we will respond in the moment by putting on filters based on our past experiences, or worse, our emotions, and believe them as fact. What we believe informs our behavior. When we are not intentionally directing our behaviors with our minds (thoughts), we allow our emotions to navigate our response, which is why so many disagreements or misunderstandings explode into something far bigger than what they started out as. The root is what we believed in that moment about our spouse or person that turned into reaction.

Talk to yourself; don't just listen to yourself. The voice inside each of us is powerful and helps us to read any given situation for both good and bad. That voice protects us, helps us avoid danger, and helps us to respond at a moment's notice. But if we don't put the narrative in order in a conflict situation with our partner, the voice can be one-sided and seemingly has one goal: self-preservation at all costs. The only way to ensure that you don't let the anger, guilt, or fear dictate your behavior is to be sure that what you tell yourself is founded in truths, not negative, punishing, protective, or defensive self talk. Talk to yourself to ensure that the behaviors that follow your inward thought life align with truths and what you choose for your life and your relationships.

Replacing negative thought patterns and self-talk is a matter of replacing those words with purpose-filled words. Words that are true. Words that speak life into a negative pattern or emotion. Creating a habit of cultivating good thoughts through speaking truths to yourself can transform how you see a situation and how you respond, and ultimately will have a lasting impact on the way you communicate with people and how you feel about communicating with people. It will have to be a consistent, intentional step by you, otherwise it is very easy to slip back into old habits of listening to thoughts that are counter to what you ultimately desire for your relationship.

The first step in talking to yourself is taking time to notice the way you currently interact with your thoughts. If you desire to have healthy communication, start between your own ears. It's an inside job. Long before another person enters the scene, how you communicate starts with the way you think. Do you typically think nice things to yourself about yourself and about your spouse, or are you unkind to yourself when you think about yourself or your person? As you begin to pay attention, you may be surprised at how much you dwell on negative or fearful thoughts or opinions that float across your mind throughout the day. By engaging with those negative thoughts, they can become a belief you hold that influences the way you view and treat your spouse, or the way you allow yourself to be treated.

In a letter written long ago to a group of people living in southeast Europe came instructions from a friend and mentor, a man by the name of Paul. If you are a Bible reader, you know him as "the apostle Paul," one of the world's most impactful evangelists and teachers to people after the time of Jesus on this earth. Known for his mastery of understanding the struggles people go through and providing practical ways to live a transformed life, Paul wrote to help his friends living in the ancient city of Philippi (now known as Greece) learn to do exactly what I'm trying to help you to do: to think in a new, healthy way. Whether or not you are a person of faith, the following excerpt is great advice for how to capture your runaway negative thoughts and instead to intentionally direct your mind to think about the good. He told them, and I say to you, "Friends, I'd say you'll do best by filling your minds and meditating on things true, noble, reputable, authentic, compelling, gracious—the best, not the worst; the beautiful, not the ugly; things to praise, not things to curse."[11] In other words, don't just fall prey to thoughts that flicker across your mind. Grab hold of your own attention and choose to see the good, not ignoring the pain, but believing the best in people as you work to communicate with both truth and love.

I talk to myself. I remind myself often what I really want from and for my life. I think about this every day. I've made it a habit to speak life to myself, both in my head and out loud. Talk to yourself. Tell yourself that you're working toward a lifelong marriage legacy because it is a relationship like no other on the planet. It's only developed in the cumulation of years of decisions to work toward one another and not apart from each other. And while you're at it, remind yourself that while this is hard, so is quitting and starting over. You can choose to do hard things that are rooted in purpose.

Assume the Best in the Other Person

I am a person who makes negative assumptions fairly easily, and I've had to work really hard to undo that habit. I like to think of assumption as discernment's evil twin. You can fool yourself into thinking that you're being discerning in a conversation, but when you build a narrative around your emotional response, you're on a slippery slope. That's not discernment at all. There's an old saying that says, "Don't assume. It makes an ass out of u and me." (Get it? ass-u-me!) The language is a little cheeky, but it reminds me that assuming is just making decisions about a person or situation in my head that may or may not be true, thus creating a belief around it that may or may not be true. Too often, I have made assumptions about KC or a particular situation. In those moments, I made generalizations instead of making observations and getting further clarification through asking questions. If I'm honest, those generalizations are typically with a negative bent, and have often been inaccurate. When I made these assumptions I was unknowingly but hastily building rocks of resentment into a wall that separated me from him emotionally in a matter of seconds. Can you relate? These negative thought rocks made the process to resolution take much longer than it needed to. It was suprising to me how quickly my mind could go from zero to one hundred when I felt wronged or hurt. Instead of assuming the worst, I needed to learn to intentionally start out believing the best in KC, and asking clarifying questions to seek further understanding.

When we believe the best in someone, they are far more apt to rise to meet the expectation when it's in their favor. We all like to be believed in and respected by another human being. The same can be applied in marriage and family relationships. As a matter of fact, it's the first place it should be applied!

When I married KC, I chose him to be my partner in life, and he chose me to be his. If you're married, you and your spouse did the same.

Shouldn't our spouse be the first person we choose to believe the best in? The home is the first place where we learn to interact and live peaceably with people who are different than us. Author Melissa Michaels put it this way: "Home is where we do the holy work of caring for our people."[12] I agree with that, but it's just the first part of the equation. We have intentionally created our home to be the place where we can depend on love, acceptance, safety, authenticity, growth, and encouragement. Where we model truth-telling, and support and love each other when we fall short. Where each of us are believed in, even when we don't yet believe in ourselves. Where boundaries are set, and healthy, regular communication is used as a tool to learn about people who are wired differently than we are, and to lovingly and skillfully restore peace when conflicts arise.

The second part of that application is when we take that love outside of our own home, to other people and their families. When we choose to love people we aren't required to love is when it gets harder; it's also when the love and "holiness" Melissa described really start to have a multiplying impact. We weren't meant to stay in a "holy huddle," only loving the people in our home. The holy work done in the home was always intended to reach outside into the world, and we start by assuming the best in others.

Talk to Others

In marriage, while assuming the best of our person is a necessary step, sometimes we need wisdom from someone outside of our marriage. Someone who has been where we are and whose relationship we respect. Some of my best learning moments have come as a result of my asking questions of others who seemed to have either intuitively done something well (within their gifting), or who worked really hard to overcome something that had held them back, and moved on to thrive. We live in a time when people are more available to us than ever. We have access to celebrities, sports figures, authors, and even world leaders, as well as business professionals and lifestyle bloggers all through our screens and social media. I can remember when my then college-aged daughter Holli got a response to her tweet from her favorite author, Bob Goff. She was over the moon! That just wasn't a possibility 20 years ago. Life through our online social hangouts and interactions has brought us closer to those we used to only admire from afar.

We also have access to regular folks who are doing life well, and with integrity. People with whom we'd ordinarily have lost track of because of a move or the busyness of life, but because of the ease of connecting through social media and smart phones, they are just a message away. It almost removes any excuses for not getting help to work through something, because so many people are accessible.

Experts and professional services are also available to us. Podcasts, blogs, LinkedIn, YouTube shows, live video on Instagram and Facebook; these are just a few ways for people to help us and show us how to do just about anything, including communicating clearly with our spouse. There are also online marriage counselors, mentors, and mentoring packages that enable anyone to have access to high quality mentoring or therapy without needing to live in geographic proximity to the counselor or mentor.

When we plug into the resources around us, we can learn to work through our communication barriers with our spouse and grow to a new place of deeper respect and understanding. I have a friend I'll call Kim, (not her real name) who went through a trying time with her husband Mike (also not his real name.) Due to the nature of their jobs and their very prominent position in their community, they were uncomfortable seeking marriage counseling locally during their marriage rough spell. They both felt uncomfortable with the idea of people in their city seeing them walking into or out of the counseling building, and reasonably so. Because of their involvement in so many different facets of community in their hometown, and not wanting to stir the gossip mill, they felt stuck. They were struggling, and yet because they felt protective of their marriage from outside opinions, they felt like they didn't have many options.

Do you feel like that sometimes? Sometimes it feels like working through something would publicly expose us in a way we aren't comfortable with, so we suffer in silence, isolating ourselves further still. Problems and trials can become magnified, and as the rock pile builds, what started as a small but problematic issue between you and your spouse can grow to become something far bigger than it ever needed to be because it was left unaddressed. Yesterday's unresolved issue is compounded by today's little miscommunication and disagreement, and they all get lumped in together until it can feel like the problems between you are insurmountable. It *feels* that way, but it's not worth letting your marriage go because it got ugly. Every marriage has ugly moments. When we let fear creep in and compound our frustration with unresolved conflict, it creates an ugly cocktail of emotion that can make things feel far worse than they are in actuality.

Fortunately, there are many options available to get help. Rather than drift away, it was important enough to both Kim and Mike to save their marriage before it really started to break down, and they chose to go looking for answers that fit their needs. My friends searched online for reputable counseling. They found one that shared their values and faith, read the referrals, and got the help they needed in the privacy of their home. If you need to talk to someone to help with a problem you can't get past, take the brave step and invite a professional in. They're out there.

Not all problems require professional help. Many just take a bit of time to resolve and then require making the decision to move away from old habits, often those that unnecessarily highlight where you're different from your spouse. Some things require time and lots of conversations during which you learn to figure one another out, which is very normal. Additionally, having someone who is further along in their marriage to give you words of wisdom can help you see your own marriage from the view a little further down the road. If you're a wife, I believe that talking with another wife who is around 10 years ahead of you in her marriage can bring peace, hope, and clarity to the stage and season of marriage that you're currently in. If you're a husband, the same goes for you. A guy who has been where you're at and discovered a healthy path to new, higher ground is such a gift. It's not typically the problems that derail the process, but your attitude about the problems. When you know people who have passed through the season you're currently in in a healthy, functional way, it helps you settle your perspective about where you're at so you can stop wondering if it can work, and find your own healthy path to a solution.

The Power of Non-Verbal Communication

While oftentimes the root of the problem is a difference of opinion or perspective, there are many times when conflict has simply been a result of misunderstanding. If I had a dollar for every time my spouse has misunderstood me, I could wallpaper my home with the bills! I am very expressive by nature, as you may have gathered. There have been many times when we have gone way off-path because I have either misrepresented my point of view or have been misunderstood. Have you ever been in a conversation that left you feeling like the person you were talking to was sending a message other than just the words they were saying? Perhaps their tone didn't align with their words, or their body language told you they were mad, even though they weren't outwardly saying so? Or maybe you've had your spouse, friend, or coworker say to you, "What was *that* supposed to mean?"

The more you communicate, the more chance there is for miscommunication. I shared a little bit about how to address a situation when you're reading someone else's tone, facial expression, or body language, but what about when it's you sending mixed or wrong signals?

Maybe you are commonly perceived as having a passive-aggressive tone of voice, a flash of annoyance on your face, or your arms folded and one foot forward when you're in a discussion; whether you mean to or not, you are sending a nonverbal signal to the person standing opposite you, and it can put the other person unnecessarily on the defense before you even say a word. You may not realize you're doing it, but it's hard for the person you love not to assume something bad is coming next when you say in a flat or agitated tone, "Can we talk?" Without asking for input from the people you love and do life with, you probably won't be aware of what it's like to be on the other side of you; experiencing your communication style, both verbal and non-verbal. If you've never thought about it before, it might feel like a lot of work to change (spoiler alert: it is a lot of work), but it can eliminate a lot of time explaining your real meaning when you can learn to be approachable and express yourself more accurately the first time. This goes both ways. We can all work on expressing ourselves in such a way that shows both visually and audibly that we want to understand and create resolution, and not to make the other person feel threatened or judged.

Have you or your spouse come home from work having had a long day, and just want to chill, but something really great happened in the other person's day that they couldn't wait to share? Maybe you said excitedly, "Babe, I had a great idea!" and your spouse looked back at you with a face that you took to mean, "Seriously, does it have to be now?" Communication is so much more than just saying words to your person. It includes learning about the power of timing, tone of voice, and body language. Because of the many methods of communicating, some that you may not have given any thought to up until now, it carries the largest weight of the 5 Cs. Communication is the main way you get through to your spouse and get on the same page as them.

In 1971, a professor at UCLA named Albert Mehrabian published two papers that discussed the research he'd done on verbal and nonverbal communication. What he found blew people's minds and continues to be used and discussed in speaking and teaching to this day. Google it later if it strikes a chord with you. It's pretty interesting. After studying a group of people, he created what is now called the "7%-38%-55% rule."[13] According to Mehrabian's research, when a person expresses themselves, the message sent is broken down into three very unequal, and probably surprising, parts. Professor Mehrabian's data showed that only 7% of what you and I communicate is solely our words. Our tone of voice, voice inflection, and pauses make up 38% of the message we're sending, while 55% of the way we connect (or don't) with people is visual: the way we stand, gesture, move our arms, and our facial expressions.

KC will openly tell you that this information is not his favorite news. When I share stuff like this with him, he feigns exhaustion (at least, I think he's feigning) and says, "Ugh. That sounds like a lot of work." He is not wrong. If we are honest, this is probably annoying and possibly overwhelming information to most of us because it means we have work to do. Work we probably never even thought of before. When we learn things like this, doesn't it make sense why so many people misunderstand one another? It's kind of amazing that relationships move forward at all. It can feel exhausting, knowing the amount of work that goes into expressing your thoughts or opinions in a healthy manner. Some personalities (mine included) thrive on this kind of information! Just tell me about it, and I'll jump right in. I think it's fun, because I'm wired relationally. Learning these kinds of facts is not anything I have to work to like—I just like it. Other people, KC included, are not naturally wired with an interest in these types of relational statistics. While KC loves me, his natural tendency is to process internally, rather than go into the weeds of all that conversation and exchange of words. I say "is," not "was," because truthfully, he still has to intentionally choose to process with me, even all these years later, because he is hardwired to process inwardly and alone. While that may have worked when it was just him, once he merged his life with mine, he chose, and continues to choose, to do the hard work of processing with a partner. Poor guy. This is anything but enjoyable for him, but because it's so important to the health of our marriage, he is willing.

For his personality, this is energy-depleting work, even as he knows it's important. Maybe you can relate to that. In fact, my mom has said for as long as I can remember, "You've got to know what I mean, not what I say!" It's not that my mom or my husband, and perhaps you, don't care about expressing themselves in a way that gets an accurate message across; the point is that it takes more work with the way they're hardwired to express outwardly in all of these ways: words, tone, and body language, and with all three sending the same message.

If you're wired like these favorite people of mine, you may be saying, "You're telling me I have to consider how the other person is wired, choose my words carefully, *and* remember to share it in the way they best receive information?" If you want a healthy relationship where your spouse feels loved? Then your answer is yes. "And now you're telling me to be cognizant of my tone of voice, the way my head is tilted, the way my arms are folded, and how I'm standing?" Truthfully, yes. That's why marriage takes a lifetime for a couple to really and wholly "merge."

It takes a long time to figure yourself out, let alone another person wired differently than you, so with an open mind and heart, give yourself and your spouse the time, the space, and a whole lot of grace to work it out. Figure out when you're at your best to have a discussion, and share that with your spouse. (Tip: for most people this is not late at night when you're both tired, so if you can avoid that, do!) Make an agreement for when you'll have the hard conversations. Maybe you're a morning person and you like a fresh mindset to do the hard work of problem-solving with your person, or maybe you think the most clearly when you're working in the garden or on a walk. Possibly you feel more comfortable having the hard conversations in an active environment, like while taking a hike, or walking along the beach, or in a calmer setting like over a cup of coffee in chairs on your front porch. Put the wind at your back by finding the right setting and time of day when you are both at your best—consider whether you feel better standing or sitting, if you like having something in your hands to fidget with, or if you like a weighted blanket on your lap. Whatever the setting is, this is your marriage, and as long as you can both agree on how, when, and where you will communicate, the key is to make the nonverbal parts of your communication as easy as possible for you.

Remember, you don't have to take the tools I'm sharing and perfect them in a month, a year, or even a decade. It takes a lifetime to discover another person, to practice with them, give one another feedback, and progress in your communication. This is why it grieves me so much when couples split up when it gets tough. It gets tough for all married people. The beauty of a lifelong marriage happens when you do the hard work of connecting again; staying with the person you promised to love, honor, and cherish "till death do you part"; choosing to fight through "the hard" of marriage; and fumbling, sometimes tearfully and sometimes laughing at yourselves. But that is where the deeper love of marriage grows. Not just in the fun times, though those times certainly are part of your story, but when you really give yourself over to the process of doing your best to speak truth with love, listen to hear the other person, and come to a place of reconciliation and resolution. Every time that happens, it strengthens your original promise.

Navigating Conflict Resolution as a Team

As you work through your communication signals, do your best not to compare yourself to others or feel less because your partner needs a little convincing. The trap might be to feel like it's too hard, or that your relationship is too far gone to save at times. There's no way of knowing that without choosing to be vulnerable and fight like crazy for what, and who, you chose. If it starts out hard, it will be all the more sweet when it turns around. Take away a finish line, stop comparing your relationship to others, cultivate hope, and stay mindful of why you're committed to this. Focus often on all the things you love about your person and how sweet it will be once you ride out the wave of tension from lack of closeness. Communicate your way to a new, deeper place of intimacy. It's worth it, trust me. If that's where you are, I've been where you are, and I cannot tell you how glad I am that neither of us quit. We would have missed out on the life we have now, and we wouldn't be the people KC and I grew into if we'd ended it when things were not at all where we hoped they'd be.

We learned to pause and clarify after one of us said something. Rather than interpret what they said through our own filters (what we think we heard, what we see in their body language, their tone of voice) and then respond accordingly, we learned to start the response with the following "I feel" and "what I hear you saying is" exercises:

- "When you say _____, I feel _____."
- "When you use that tone of voice, I feel _____."
- "When you stand like that, I feel like you're sending me the message that _____."
- "When you said _____, what I heard was _____."

Are you with me? Sometimes, it took us forever to simply get to the issue at hand because we misinterpreted one another's body language, tone of voice, and facial expressions; these things blocked the message the other was sending because one of us responded emotionally due to our filters. More often than not, we had read one another all wrong. This was exhausting, and many times we were both so frustrated or mad that we took breaks to cool off in an effort to try to stay respectful. We didn't always accomplish that in the early days, as we had a long way to go. My way was to talk it to death; and KC's way was to clam up and shut the conversation down because it was uncomfortable and his emotional negative filter took over. Then we'd come back and go another round. Truthfully the large majority of our arguments were just the struggle of trying to figure one another out, and when we'd completely misread each other. Once we got past the visual and auditory communication errors, we were actually able to solve most issues pretty quickly. Sometimes we just had to let it sit, agree to disagree in that moment (more on that next chapter), and choose to heal the relationship so we could move forward.

We were both pretty good at saying "I'm sorry" for our part and extending forgiveness to the other when they apologized. That may be a struggle for you, and if it is, let me assure you that it is common, and it can be learned. Pride is a hard one to overcome, but once you get the hang of humbling yourself to say "I'm sorry" and "I forgive you," you've just won a large portion of the battle within yourself. Choosing to be vulnerable enough to admit when you've been wrong or have hurt the other person, rather than harboring grudges or hanging onto anger, enables you to prepare your heart to forgive your spouse when they've been wrong or have hurt you. The faster you can get to that place where you are open to healing and releasing the emotion for the sake of fully reconciling, the healthier your relationship becomes.

We all argue and have disagreements and different viewpoints on a variety of topics, but keeping the end goal in mind helps you to avoid unnecessarily pouring emotional gasoline on the fire with your words and actions. After all, is our goal to win the argument or to fix the problem? Have you ever been so mad that you know your response is irrational, and somewhere along the line it stopped being about the subject you're discussing and more about letting off a little steam? This can be detrimental to the relationship and can leave your spouse feeling attacked or emotionally unsafe to be vulnerable for fear that you'll trample over their feelings. Remind yourself often what my friend, author Doug Fitzgerald, says: "Your spouse is not your enemy." I'm sure you'd say that you know that, but do you sometimes treat them like they are?

Years ago, one of our sons was playing youth soccer. Joseph was caught up in the game, totally "in the zone" but hadn't yet learned the nuances of soccer. This kid played to win. In fact, one of his coaches nicknamed him "see ball, get ball." Though he was happy to be on a team, it took him a couple years to play like he was. When he got in the game, he just wanted to get the ball, dribble through all the players, and score the goal. We sat on the sidelines one Saturday and saw him spring into action. Joseph got that cute look of intensity on his face, and with focus and athletic assertiveness, he went after the player with the ball, took it with gusto, and headed for the goal. It was a great play, but no one cheered. There was awkward silence on the side of the field for a moment because the kid who had the ball . . . the one Joseph took it from . . . was his teammate. We were the parents of *that kid*. Thankfully the other parents on our team started to laugh, but KC and I were shouting to Joseph in what he thought was his moment of glory, "Joseph! Same team! That's your teammate!"

It's a funny childhood moment, but this can be similar to when we are trying to come to resolution with our spouse. Often, husbands and wives just haven't learned the nuances of problem-solving in their marriage, so we go to the closest thing we know: sports. Two teams, one winner. But marriage isn't a sport, and the goal isn't to win; you are both playing for the same team. To love and respect one another in the process is far more important than the issue at hand. You're on the same team; you're not each other's opposition. The goal is resolution as a team. And in the grand scheme of life, is what you're arguing about so important that you'll even remember it a year from now? Or next month? Or even next week? Perspective is a powerful thing in an argument with your spouse. If you're getting upset, pause, step back from the issue, look into the face of the person you're going to head-to-head with, remember that you love and value the person, and remind yourself: same team.

> **The goal isn't to win; you are both playing for the same team.**

Back in 1990 when we were in pre-marriage mentoring, we learned a healthy formula for approaching tough conversations that KC and I now teach in our own marriage mentoring. I'm going to share it with you and hope you master putting this into action better and sooner than I did. You or your spouse may slip sometimes, which is to be expected. It's just part of learning a new way of communicating. This formula takes intentionality, and it will take self-discipline to make it a part of the way you interact.

When bringing up a potentially lengthy or touchy discussion, consider the following tips:

1. Do so in a way that is disarming, and with the end result in mind.
2. Don't approach the other person when emotional; wait until a calmer head prevails.
3. Don't use phrases like "you always" and "you never." No one does anything "always" or "never," and because of the accusatory nature, this puts your person immediately on the defense.
4. No one can "make" another person feel or do anything. What happens to us is out of our control, but our response to what happens is up to us. Own your own thoughts, emotions, and responses.

Let me give you a personal example of how not to approach the conversation. When we were first married, I chose an issue that I was dissasfied with that I wanted to discuss with KC. I'd gotten myself all worked up with poor self-talk about him ahead of time and was pretty mad when I stepped in front of the TV as he watched the news after work. I had my rocks and was ready to use them; he had no idea he was about to be ambushed. "I want to talk to you about something," I said in an angry tone, giving in to my emotion both from the situation at hand and the emotional anticipation of the topic (Strike One).

He looked up, paused the TV, and said, "What?" To me, his facial expression looked more like, "What now?" This fueled my frustration, and through my filter, confirmed the feelings I'd been mentally cataloging as facts.

"You have really been hurting my feelings lately," I said (Strike Two). "You always watch TV after work"—(Strike Three)—"instead of spending time with me. You know it offends me," I continued (Strike Four), "and I think you're ignoring that on purpose because you don't want to change it. You've made me feel"—(Strike Five)—"so isolated lately!"

I nearly struck out for myself twice in my opening statement alone. Aargh! In those days I didn't know better, and a healthy conversation didn't stand a chance with that poor setup. I had missed the purpose and goal: which was to express something I was feeling, address the root issue, and collaborate together on a plan to move forward that worked for both of us. Healthy and functional communication took a while to develop in our relationship, and though my approach that day stunk, I had to learn to pause to ask myself what I ultimately wanted. You'll want to do the same. For me, what I desired deep down was for us to be more intentionally close and connected by spending more time together. There's no way he could have received that message from what I said. Author Andy Stanley says it this way: "A communicator's approach to communicating must be in support of the overall goal."[14] I put KC on the defense right from the start, and I actually brought about the opposite of what I ultimately wanted. It didn't go well, obviously. Blasting the other person might feel good for the moment as you release pent-up frustration in a blast of emotion-fueled words, but it opens up a whole other issue about respectful conflict resolution that now will need to be addressed and worked through before the original conversation can happen. In short, it's completely counter to what we want. Remember: same team. This step alone may change a lot of what's not connecting between the two of you. It really did for us.

The other thing we learned and now teach is not to exaggerate. Eliminate phrases like, "You make me feel this way when you say that!" or, "You always make me feel bad when you do this . . ." Instead, look for a positive, non-aggressive, non-accusatory way to express yourself: "When you say the kitchen is a mess, I feel like what you're really saying is I should have cleaned it. Is that what you mean?" or, "When you know you need to work late and don't call or text to let me know, it feels like you're not respecting my feelings or our time together." For us and so many couples that we've mentored, learning to practice these simple changes in the way we communicate made it far easier to stick to the issue at hand rather than making a mountain out of a mole hill, butting heads and feeling disconnected and misunderstood.

Start the Conversation

Okay. You've taken your first steps toward personal assessment and responsibility of your thoughts, assumptions, and beliefs. You might be surprised to have learned how you are visibly perceived in communication and conflict resolution. You might be finding that you have some work to do, and recognizing the same in your spouse. This is a lifelong process; one conversation won't reveal everything that needs to be revealed, as learning about yourself and your spouse is a long game; but it will start you on a path that will help you develop a life-long habit of evaluation and course correction. Perfection shouldn't be your goal—instead, strive to take a small step forward. Progress is absolutely attainable! It will take time to learn how to relate to one another and, to some degree, will be like peeling an onion. People are complex and simple at the same time, so as you begin to unpeel the layers of your person *with* your person, settle into the process and keep moving forward together. Bring your thoughts and hopes to the table of discussion with your spouse. This is where you begin to build the first of many game plans together!

In Chapter One, I had you take your assessments and discuss them on a date or series of dates; some great conversation may have been sparked then. This next bit is a natural next step for you to assess all the things you have chosen separately and/or together that you want your marriage and family to look like, and then discuss the steps you will take to prioritize those choices. These are big topics where you should choose a long-term goal and proceed with the following Cs. Life will morph, and you will both grow and change over time; so will the way your goals actualize. You'll want to continue returning to the Cs as you grow, so your action plan grows with you and your life changes.

I don't recommend approaching your intro conversation while in a fight, or when you are upset with one another. In order for this to go well, you'll want it to start off well, and that requires choosing the proper timing and mindset to sit down to discuss things. This can be a really fun, "big dream" kind of talk, but if you're in a tough place presently, you may want to invite in either a trusted mentor couple or even a marriage and family therapist who comes highly recommended. No shame in that. We've been there before in the early years, and we've also been the mentor couple for others in that spot.

Your spouse may or may not have believed there was anything to change, or maybe even has felt a little defensive, suspicious that you might be using this as an opportunity to try to change them. Either way, go into this conversation prepared to love your partner through to understanding. No one can change another person, so stay focused on your own growth. Your goal is to use these 5 Cs to grow together and make your relationship the best it can be in each season of marriage. Not to be right, or to fix the other person. It's okay if you have to do a gut check if that was your underlying motive to start. That's part of the process for yourself: letting go of controlling the outcome and instead committing to a process. Your spouse knows you, and your motives will be transparent in these kinds of talks. You might hope for different behaviors or ways of interacting, but if you go in with an underlying hope to change your spouse, it will be counterproductive. How many times has someone else changed you by pointing out your weaknesses and telling you how much better things would be if you just changed some things? Think of how hard it is to change yourself. Why would we ever think we can change someone else? Our motives must be for the betterment of the relationship, not to change the other person. The benefit is that of course, you will grow and change as individuals as each of you opens your mind to becoming the next best version of yourself—then, you can create the marriage you desire.

To open your first big conversation, you might start out approaching your spouse by saying something like, "Remember when I said I was interested in us being more intentional about our relationship? Well, I've been doing some inward self-awareness steps and motive checks, getting my thoughts together, and would love to talk to you about it when we can both be uninterrupted. And, baby"—(insert your pet name if you have one with a smile and sweet voice)—I am excited about this, so please keep an open mind!" Say it in your own words and in your own way. Come unarmed to this conversation if you want to continue it! Change is hard. It's even harder when it comes when you're not expecting it, so just be sure to be positive, loving, and patient.

Because of my family background, I had an idea of what I wanted our marriage and family to look like. Combined with the things that I wanted to do differently, there were some things I knew I wanted to purposefully implement in our family. I shared with KC my thoughts and asked if he was willing, open, and interested in talking about how we could pursue those things in our marriage. KC definitely had the desire, I had the vision, and we had to find our way just like you and your spouse will find your way. No two marriages look the same, nor would we want them to! It's the beauty of our differences that makes each marriage its own unique story. We could all implement a date night, for instance, and they would all look different, because of our interests, personalities, sense of humor, expectations, and experiences. One couple may enjoy playing board games at home, another might love going out to eat and to a play, while a third might think a rowdy game of Ping-Pong sounds like the perfect couple's evening. That's why we should never compare, only work to be the best version of ourselves that we can be. I hope you find that thought as freeing as I do!

Once you sit down with your spouse to process your big vision together, get some blank paper or open a new document on a tablet. Talk about what each of you would like your marriage and possibly eventual family to look like in the long term and write down both of your ideas. Here are some examples that I'll share to get your creative juices started:

- I would like us to have more regular, open communication.
- I would like our marriage relationship to take more center stage in our family.

- I would like to set some boundaries with your/my/both of our parents.
- I feel like we aren't as close as we could be. Could we talk about some ways to intentionally spend more time together?
- I feel like screens (phones, tablets, computers, TVs, video games) have taken over a lot of free time. Can we talk about maybe setting up some boundaries around our free time together?
- I need more help with the kids' schedules. Can we work out a system so we can work more efficiently, and as a team?
- I would love to have a regular date night and family night.
- I would like to have sex more often, or discuss our sex life more regularly.
- I feel like our interactions need to be more respectful. I own my part in that. Can we please discuss having boundaries for the way we talk to one another (e.g., sarcasm, name calling, or cursing)?
- I believe we are on very different pages regarding money. I'd love to set up a budget that we can both agree to.
- I want us to create a strong family culture so by the time we have kids, they'll want to be home in their teen years. What might that look like, practically?

Those are a few to get you going. Remember, this first conversation of many to come is about discovering what you both envision for your marriage in the big picture. But it can also be about how to navigate the little day-to-day things in a productive way as they come along. Have fun with it. If one is more the visionary than the other, that's okay, let the one with the vision share and leave space for the other to add to it once sparked and bring their honest response to the vision. Ideally, you've discussed much of this before marriage, but if not, there's no better time than the present to start dreaming and communicating about how you want your marriage and family to play out. This isn't a "one-and-done" conversation; it might take several conversations to work through the WHAT before you get to the HOW (more on this in the next chapter), but this is your life. Make the time to flesh it out. The goal is to get comfortable talking together about where you're going.

Even if this conversation takes a few rounds, don't be discouraged. Think of how long it takes to make any changes in your own life as an individual. And now you're trying to live out the merging of two lives into one marriage. Building a marriage for life is a "long game"; it's a marathon, not a sprint. Lean into the process of conversation and know that what you're doing is the sometimes hard and often fun, but always meaningful, work of creating the life you truly desire.

Key Choices

Years ago, KC and I found a great marriage and family therapist when one of our kids needed some outside help with coping skills, and it turned out to be a surprising blessing to our marriage. We have since met with her several times over the years in order to learn more about ourselves and gain insights that have given us quite a boost in using our marriage tools. Not everyone goes to see a marriage therapist or attends a marriage weekend retreat because they are in crisis. You might consider giving your marriage a concentrated boost of tools and togetherness by attending a series of therapy sessions with a local or online marriage therapist or mentor, or sign up for a weekend getaway or marriage retreat to work on your marriage. These events are designed to help you build healthy communication in your marriage, and you get a little vacation out of the event! Win-win!

Action Steps:

1. Schedule a date in a place where you can both talk freely. Address any gaps that have been left undiscussed. Bring a notebook or tablet to write out your thoughts. It may be uncomfortable and may trigger an argument if there are current gaps in your communication, but that's okay. Hang with it. You need to learn one another's conversational rhythms. Begin with the mindset that you want to discuss this not to win against your spouse, but to win together! If you need to do this in steps, that's okay. There are no rules. This is about taking your current relationship and making it better, and sometimes it gets messy before it gets cleaned up if you're not in a healthy place right now. Try to end on a positive note. Acknowledge the progress you've made and commit to creating something you both love.

2. Write out a whole list of things together, based on what you'd like your marriage to look like. Have fun with it! Access as many of your senses as possible on your creative date so it's something to look forward to. Time together should be intentionally fun for both of you.

BONUS: If you're feeling like you're making good progress together, you may want to tackle a separate list for how you'd like to interact and connect with your kids if you have them. Your kids are the second tier in your family relationships, after your marriage. This is where your relationship model starts to work its way toward making a mark in the world, through relationships outside the home. Have fun with the list. Lean into your individual strengths as parents. Together, you can complement one another in how you will uniquely train up this growing little human or tribe of humans.

Collaboration is Key

The greatest marriages are designed and created as a team.

Collaboration, the third C, is how you intentionally create the marriage you desire through your actions. These actions bind you together to form a matchless marriage, unlike any other on the planet. The greatest marriages are designed and created as a team, over time, with many choices and behaviors to back those choices over a lifetime. It takes courage to create something you've never seen before, to take brave steps toward the desired but unknown. It takes determination to start again without blaming one another when something isn't working just right, humility to take ownership of your part of the equation, and fierce loyalty to take steps back toward one another over and over again as your choices create something new. There will be rewards in the collaboration, as your choices compound with every new choice. It will take work, but it's work that will directly benefit you and your kids and their kids, for generations to come. And it will serve as a guide for others that great marriages are possible for them too.

Co-Creators

They say that creativity is one of the deepest yearnings of the human soul. You might have thought of that as artwork in the traditional sense, on a canvas or with clay, but I believe it's also deep in the heart of people to create lasting, healthy, lifelong family relationships.

As you work to co-create your marriage, the two of you get to intentionally design the marriage and family relationships that you both desire. You get to collaborate on a plan that is a unique fit for both of you, take the things you want to experience in your marriage, and work on a plan that is acceptable and manageable. It's exciting!

Once you've established core foundational building blocks on which you desire to build your relationship, you can now put them in place. Keep in mind that as you collaborate on how this will initially be put into play, sometimes life will call on you to tweak the plan. Expect change and circumstances to occur and have the expectation that your approach may need adjustment along the way.

If you struggled to get to this point because too many conflicts have gone unresolved to the point that it hinders a fun conversation about the growth of your relationship, it might be time to consider getting marriage mentoring or counseling. Just put a pause here to get those conflicts resolved. Sometimes KC and I had to do that. Many times our disputes were inconsequential and a matter of two different viewpoints. This is when we chose to do something we called "agreeing to disagree." On these occasions, the outcome didn't affect our marriage as a whole, but was a mildly annoying minor point of friction. I'm sure you have these as well, or you will. Agreeing to disagree says that we can both keep our views and still move forward without carrying the friction into future conversations. Your spouse is entitled to her opinion, and you are to yours, and you don't need to change either of your stances in order to move forward in peace.

On the other side of that spectrum, I can also think of three occasions where KC and I were blocked in our communication and collaboration, unable to come to resolution. Trying to move forward was unproductive because we saw things so differently in areas that really had an impact on our marriage. These issues made a negative impact on us for several days, and every time we tried to resolve it with communication (the second C) we could not collaborate on a plan to resolve it, as we disagreed so sharply. It was during those times that we chose to invite our mentors in. Once we even invited a trusted pastor friend in for input. Sharing a very personal struggle with a mentor or pastor is uncomfortable, particularly for me, but it was a critical step toward healing.

Back then, KC was much more open than I was in this area. Each time we have reached for help outside the home has taught me something about myself. Each time shined a light on areas that needed work. If you are uncomfortable with this idea, believe me, I understand. I am a very private person. For as open as I am on social media and with my love for people and sharing my life, there is a very private side of me that I don't share with anyone but my immediate family and closest friends. Those are the most vulnerable, bare parts, but also the raw, undeveloped parts of me that adversity reveals pretty quickly. If things are not going well with me, or in my relationships, I like to keep those cards very close to my chest and out of the public eye. I don't mind sharing after we've had resolution, but there is no way I am going to share an open wound publicly before it's resolved. This preserves the privacy of our marriage, but it also works against me when I need help.

On one hand, it's important to keep private matters private. I am extremely protective of KC and the opinions others have of him. I think it's important for a husband or wife to guard the reputation of their spouse by showing one another respect in front of others. I don't mean hiding dangerous or damaging behaviors that require professional help; I'm talking about weaknesses and failings that are common to humanity. If I let my pride get the best of me, I can be isolated quickly if I am at an impasse with my marital relationship and am not willing to share my burdens with trusted people in a safe environment for fear of being judged or misunderstood. There is a fine line between being open but appropriately protective, and pretending in order to protect one's perceived reputation of perfection. I have learned through the years how to share a personal struggle without feeling like I'm throwing my loved ones under the bus or infringing on their privacy. I've also learned how to be transparent enough that people watching see an authentic, purpose-filled life lived out loud. People *are* watching—honestly, aren't we all watching to see how others are making it work in life, and to see whose lives are worth emulating, and whose words are aligned with their behaviors?

> There is a fine line between being open but appropriately protective, and pretending in order to protect one's perceived reputation of perfection.

The other thing I have learned through personal experience with trial is that using discernment in whom we allow to help with resolution is critical. If you're at an impasse of your own and are nervous to invite someone into your most personal relationship, I believe that it's wise to trust your instinct; asking the wrong person for advice at a critical time of vulnerability can have devastating results. As I mentioned before, I once had a friend give me off-base advice with the best of intentions, and at a pretty sensitive season in my marriage. But because I had clearly identified what I wanted from and for my marriage, I was able to discern that it was not good advice. This is why a good, highly recommended marriage and family therapist is a good alternative if you don't yet have a mentor couple. A pastor or clergy member who has a counseling background (not all of them do!) is another good option. For us, we were able to talk with our pastor about what our struggle was on this one occasion, and it was exactly the breakthrough we needed.

When KC and I had been married for five or six years, we had three kids and were very involved at our church. At that time, our church, like many organizations, functioned with about 20% of the people doing 80% of the work. KC and I were in that 20%. KC is one of the most service-oriented people I've ever met. He's that guy who sees the need before most. He notices the job no one wants to do, and he just does it without calling attention to himself. He enjoys doing this and typically gets little to no recognition, and he's perfectly comfortable with that. It's one of his most admirable traits. Sometimes, especially in the early days, if he didn't run every opportunity through the filter of his priorities and talk about it with me, he might have ended up spending all of his free time away from home, serving others with joy but out of balance.

That's where we were at, way back when. He was spread thin and our relationship was showing it. He had signed up to mentor an at-risk teen in our community and was spending free time on the weekends helping an elderly lady who had some home projects that needed to be done. In addition to that, we were the junior high youth pastors of the church, and KC was the sole person who set up and broke down the coffee station at church every Sunday morning. Our three kids were under age four, and I was pregnant with our fourth child. Our life was full; yes, full of fun and love and all that goes with raising a sweet growing family, but also with the commitments we'd made to the people we were serving at church and in the community.

We were maxed out, and I felt it first. In a lot of ways I felt like I was doing it alone with the kids, but we were both conflicted because what KC was doing was helping people who needed help. I would complain as he'd leave, yet feel guilty because he was doing such good work for people who genuinely needed it and who were so grateful for his time. KC felt that if he had a spare moment, he was compelled to use it to help people who needed help; and there was no shortage of people who needed help. We would go round and round in emotionally charged discussions. (Arguments.) In those days he was working long hours so we could afford for me to be a stay-at-home-mom with our kids, and in addition to his regular job, he cleaned an office building once a week as a side hustle. It's not hard to see why we had tension. It wasn't realistic for the long-term. He felt like I wasn't appreciating his hard work, and I felt like he wasn't home enough. I wanted him to serve less so he could be home with me and the kids more, and he felt like we had been blessed with so much, how could he turn away opportunity to help people with less?

We couldn't get to a place where we could both feel comfortable with "the plan." Finally, when we'd gone around for what felt like the twentieth time on the topic, I asked him if he would be interested in talking to our pastor, a trusted guy who I felt might be a good resource as he was a married dad of four who was both pro-marriage and pro-service. It seemed like he was the right person to help us settle the issue that was taking up way too much of our conversations, and joy, recently. KC agreed.

When our pastor and friend agreed to meet with us, we sat in his office and explained why we needed an intercessor. We needed him: a friend who knew us well, but also knew our priorities and values and faith well enough to weigh in on the topic. He heard us and helped us collaborate on a plan that served our family, but also allowed KC to serve in his giftings and passion. By listening to us, really hearing us, he helped us take back control of how we were choosing to use our time. He helped KC to see that while he was designed and gifted to serve, the first people he was to serve well were his family. Don't get me wrong. KC wanted to be with us, but he was also in tune to the weight of the need around us, and that triggered his desire to do more. Without an outside opinion from someone we both trusted to, in effect, give him "permission" to have free family time guilt-free while needs still went unmet out in the world, it would have been really hard for KC to stop spending all of his free time out serving.

We needed that permission for KC to draw back a little, and then to collaborate with me to draw boundaries around established family time and specified time for him to serve others. When the order of our priorities and calendar is in line with our goals, then we can say no to perfectly noble and good things because we have organized our priorities into agreed-upon time blocks for service. This doesn't have to be your issue for you to capture the lesson. So many of us have things we feel strongly about, but it all comes back to collaborating— together—on a plan to organize the time allotted for the things the matter. Same team.

Nonnegotiables

Every couple is different from the next. We come from different backgrounds, have different experiences, and are a unique combination of personality, giftings, interests, and observations from those experiences. This next part will look different for each couple, which is really the fun of this next exercise: determining through collaboration what priorities are "nonnegotiables" for your relationship. I made a list to help get you thinking of what you really want your marriage and family to look like. You will notice that the things we chose focused around not only being a couple but raising a family. We had our first baby two and a half years after we got married, so the priorities we chose for our relationship translated pretty quickly into how they would work and assimilate in a family setting. Maybe you've never thought out exactly what you want; perhaps up till now you have had a sort of ambiguous ideal marriage in your mind that wasn't ever detailed out. And maybe you even held your real-life marriage up to that undefined illusion of a perfectly satisfying marriage and found it lacking. That's not abnormal, but it's not helpful either. I want to help you define your ideal marriage—together—so you have an actual measurable goal to work toward. And whether that includes children or not can all be a part of this step of collaborating.

To get you started, here are some of the ways we put into place our top priorities that supported our overall goals for our marriage. While these are some of the things we considered nonnegotiables, yours might be different and that's okay. The goal is to define and then create the marriage and family that fits you and your person. Remember to read these for the purpose of viewing a snapshot of one couple's story, and to get a picture of what you may (or may not) want for your own marriage. I'm not sharing it because we did everything perfectly; God knows we didn't. I'm sharing so you can get an idea of one way to do things, and for it to hopefully instigate some great collaboration for you and your person.

Make Regular Time for One Another

At the top of my and KC's list of nonnegotiables was having a date night. When we were newly married, date night was a priority, but it was irregular. It's something I wish we'd done differently, but that's the beauty of hindsight. For many couples, in the early years of marriage, they have more free time, but money is tight. If you choose to have a family, as you're having and raising kids, your commitments expand and your income has to be stretched to meet needs. Over time, your circumstances shift to where you have a bit more money, but your time is short. Then there are those seasons in between when you don't feel like you have either time or money. That's how it was with us. We found quickly that if we wanted to spend time together regularly, it was going to have to be intentional, as there would never be what felt like a "perfect time."

Back then, there were no social media influencers (because there was no social media), so even the term "date night" with your spouse wasn't much of a social norm. Still, we were advised in our marriage prep class to get alone as much as possible to stay connected. Early marriage dates were more spread out back then, and we either went out alone, or with a group of friends of other married couples we went to church with and did life with. These dates were so good for us to stay connected, have fun together, and keep the romance alive.

Finding other couples in your age and stage of life is so important for the health of your marriage. We knew some couples who didn't really find couples to connect with early on, so they did their best to maintain their individual friendships and activities with their single friends. From our experience, this typically causes more separation than togetherness and doesn't do much for redefining yourselves as a couple. I'm not saying you give up your friends just because they're single, but there is a natural separation that occurs simply by nature of where you are each at in your lives. You see one another less frequently purely due to the difference in activities you did as single person versus what you now do socially as a married person. We advise young couples to be intentional to forge new bonds with a few couples they both enjoy. It's so helpful when you have people in a similar place in life to go through this new stage with—people who get what you're going through and who can support you in times where you're figuring this new phase out. Our couple friends back then were such an important part of our journey, both relationally and socially, and we are still friends with a few of those couples all these years later.

Back in those early days we didn't have a lot of money, and it seemed we were always working on a home improvement project around our house because our first home was a fixer-upper. We worked together and enjoyed that time doing something that was for us and our future family. We had dates alone and some with our best friends (my sister and brother-in-law.) In the early years, I think we got together with them at least one night nearly every weekend. They'd been married for nine years when we got married, so eventually when we had our first baby, their four kids, our nieces and nephew, were about ten years older than our baby and were wonderful free babysitters. We quickly went from newlywed stage to full-blown family life as we had our first four babies in a short span of five years. We would go to my sister's house to hang out, and the cousins would scoop up our kids and take them upstairs to play with them. We were really fortunate in that way because we had adult conversation regularly, and guilt-free because our kids looked forward to being with the cousins.

If you choose to not have children for a while, you'll have more time to adjust to life as a couple, but no matter when you decide to have kids, there is an adjustment period with each new stage. We went from dates alone, to walking with a baby in a stroller, to walking around the block in our neighborhood for an inexpensive date as our kids became old enough to be home on their own for just a short bit. Because we were youth pastors for a little over a decade, we also had our pick from the teens at church to be our sitters, and when our own older kids came of age to babysit the younger siblings for the evening, we confirmed Friday as our official date night, and it's been that way for the last fifteen years and counting.

In the early years before I was bringing in a regular income, our budget was small for such a large family, our time was limited, and our energy was usually spent by evening time. But Fridays... Fridays were our time together, and back in the day when our budget didn't allow for a babysitter *and* dinner, we'd just sit in our backyard and talk, and let the kids have a "special treat": watch a movie and have a picnic dinner in the living room. We'd borrow a cute family movie from the local library or from a friend and pop it into the VCR while they ate dinner on a blanket on the floor. Food was normally off-limits in the living room, so we made a big deal out of them being old enough to have a living room picnic. We told them they could interrupt us with important questions or if someone was hurt or in danger (we were just outside the sliding back doors), but Mommy and Daddy were on a date. This put up a boundary around our time together from the time they were young; intentionally building date night into the fabric of our family culture. When they were young, our kids were always so good during these dates because it was special for them too. They looked forward to Friday nights like it was their own! By intentionally creating an out-of-the norm experience for them, we eliminated a lot of pushback right from the beginning. By letting them do something that felt a little grown-up (eating in the living room, sometimes with a little candle in a glass on the coffee table), we in turn got an uninterrupted cheap date alone, mostly.

As our big kids became teens, and our income grew and allowed us to go out to actual restaurants for our dates, all throughout high school the kids respected the night we went out—no doubt because it had been a part of our family culture for as long as they could remember. We bought pizza for them, their friends, and their younger siblings who they were babysitting for free, so there would be something fun in it for them (still working the "special treat" angle), and we headed out to sit and have one quiet meal a week together to talk and connect as a couple. It was always dinner, sometimes a movie too, but we rarely ever went to a movie only. We met to spend time not just next to each other staring at a screen, but to talk to each other. This kept us connected and regularly clearing the air. As the main purpose of our once-a-week date was to hang out together regularly, stay connected, and kick off each weekend by resolving any issues, that sometimes meant we went out to bicker. I mean, it's not like we planned to argue over a meal, but because it was our regular catch-up time for the week, it just naturally turned out that way. It stinks when date night becomes "dinner and an argument" instead of "dinner and a movie," but it's also real life and how healthy communication works.

I loved how our kids honored our date night. While in high school, if one of them wanted to make plans for Friday, they talked amongst each other to make sure one of them would be home with the younger siblings. As we all grew up and our littles turned into young adults, it was fun to invite them to join us for a double date so we could get to know them and the person they were seriously dating. I think a regular date night is one of the most, if not *the* most, consistent things we've done throughout our marriage. The return on that time/money/ emotional investment has paid back a thousand-fold. This has been the bedrock of our staying connected over the years. I meet so many parents who feel guilty to leave their kids, some that flat out won't leave them, and many make the trusty "who has time" excuse. The truth is, none of us has the time, and *all* of us can and need to make the time for a weekly date to nurture the most important relationship in the family.

You might think it's bizarre—maybe even wrong—to hear me say that the marriage is the most important relationship in the family, especially if you haven't seen that done well. I certainly don't mean that if and when you bring children into the mix you should treat them as second class citizens, but we've seen far too many marriages where once children come on the scene, the wife checks out emotionally with her husband and goes all-in on mom-ing, neglecting her marriage in the process. More than likely, this is a result of the 5 Cs not having been utilized before baby came onto the scene, and as the mommy-baby bond fills an emotional need in the mom, it can cause resentment in the husband and distance in the marriage. Yes, those babes are precious and need our care, love, and training, but too many times if you're not careful, that's the point where the marriage takes a back seat to parenting. In that season where the days are long and the years are short, it's not uncommon for a couple to drift apart in the busyness of life. And one day you can seemingly wake up, look at one another as your kids are headed off to college and have no connection apart from those kids. If you happen to be reading this and are at that point, it's not too late. You can reconnect again! Beginning by reimagining your future, owning your part in the disconnect, and rebuilding step by step with this book: together. If you still have it all before you, you are aware of the potential pitfalls and can chart your course by being intentional to stay connected. Remember if you have children, that parenting is raising up babies into grown-ups who will hopefully add to society in a positive and productive way as they create their own life, career, marriage, and family. They will not stay forever if you do it well. They will launch into their own future and family. Your spouse, God-willing, will stay for the long haul. It's the relationship that goes the distance. In a study of the family unit, The Center For Law and Social Policy found that kids whose parents have a healthy marriage statistically do better in school, are less likely to live below the poverty level, are less likely to get pregnant outside of marriage, and are less prone to having behavioral and psychological problems.[15] In other words, when a marriage is healthy, it creates an environment for healthy children who have the statistical advantage of becoming healthy adults.

Long before we had children, I read a statement that surprised me and caused me to pause and reflect. It said, "The greatest gift a father can give his children is to love their mother." Wow. Now don't read too much into what this is saying. In context, it is saying that absolutely, fathers need to love their children, and help provide a safe and loving childhood for them, one where they are instructed as they develop and where they are believed in. All those good and important fatherly things. But when a father loves their mother, it establishes an order within the home that provides emotional safety, stability, and security for kids to reach their highest potential without the worries of their parents' marriage and disruption in the home. Ideally, healthy relationships within a marriage show our sons how to love, respect, and treat their future wives; and show our daughters how a woman loves and respects her husband and can expect to be treated by their own future husband one day. It positions the parents as a team, united before the kids, with the marriage as the central relationship "hub" of the family. That is a big perk of the investment in making time together a priority. You can better operate as a united front when you are actually regularly "united" and really spending time together, not just running the business side of the family. By investing in a healthy marriage and a healthy family culture, your odds greatly increase for releasing well-adjusted young people into adulthood, who in turn help make this world a better place. It's why we are so passionate about it. We believe that when we change the health of our marriages and families, we change the world, one family at a time.

Schedule Daily, Relational "Upkeep" Conversations

KC and I probably didn't start "upkeep" conversations as early as we should have. We soon realized that in order to maintain relational health, we needed to set aside regular time daily for us to connect. This is the power of using these tools; they weave into and feed on one another; they aren't linear, when once you've completed a step, you then move on to the next and don't look back. No, part of making sure that the plan is working like we want it to requires upkeep conversations. Take it from me, if you set this up from the beginning, you'll be glad you did. Before you get married, you are more apt to have the daily upkeep conversations because you intentionally planned when you'd see each other. Like most dating or engaged couples, after work or school each day you most likely planned to spend time together. Time where each of you would share about your day, ask questions about the other's day, and share upcoming events that you've been invited to or fun things you want to do when you're together next. It probably wasn't a lot of work because you missed each other during the day, and depending on how long you dated before marriage, you may have put real life things on the back burner. Things like paying bills, cleaning your living space, and washing your car may have become background noise as you fell in love and spent as much time as possible with your person. KC and I marvel at how we hardly got sleep back in those early days when we'd talk for hours in the months leading up to the wedding. It is an amazing experience, falling in love. You really do live in a love bubble.

And then you get married, and you settle in to the fun new norm of not needing to schedule time to see one another because you live in the same space. All of those dreamy conversations talking about your pasts, your present, and your future together can slip into the back seat while real life and the tyranny of the urgent takes front seat. The honeymoon ends, and you settle into your new norm, including all the things that seemingly come into the light after the wedding, when the next stage of marriage becomes a bit more real. The dreamy haze of pre-marital love and passion sharpens into reality. It is simultaneously fun to live in the same space as husband and wife and is also a learning curve where habits and idiosyncrasies spring to life. Or maybe they were always there, and you just missed them? Either way, as you settle into the fun of being Mr. and Mrs. and forever roommates, it's also strange how little differences suddenly feel spotlighted: seemingly benign little things like a bath towel lying on the floor, a water glass leaving a ring on the coffee table, dishes in the sink, and an unmade bed suddenly are annoying daily talking points.

Because of our differences, and perhaps you'll find this too, in those early days there was a lot of friction. You may find this surprising, especially if you felt like you hardly ever bickered before you got married. Once we settle into the day-to-day living as husband and wife, if we aren't careful, we can disconnect pretty easily, without even intending to. I think it's interesting to find that while it takes a lot of work to stay connected, it's very easy to become distracted and distanced from one another by treating your marriage like a business exchange.

Truthfully, these little distractions and bickerings are very normal. Remember when you shared a room with a sibling, or got a new roommate in your college or single life? It takes time to acclimate to another person's way of doing things and to find a rhythm between you two. It's the same with marriage. Allow the space to get used to one another, acknowledge where it is challenging and at the same time normal, and know that it's part of the whole wonderfully messy package of marriage. Trust one another and keep your conversations respectful and productive as you learn to coexist with your person as co-owners of the same space.

On top of all that, when too much time goes by between conversations about things that matter, light-hearted, flirty banter can become non-existent between the two of you. Make intentional time to be in one another's space, talking about the things you used to talk about, as well as the nuances of marriage as they present themselves. Life is busy, and it might happen that one or both of you are avoiding the conversations about your partnership where you disagree. I know it might feel easier to ignore these issues or sweep them under the carpet, but in the end, issues left unaddressed become bigger over time and eventually get to the point where they must be addressed. Take it from me, the sooner you talk about the things that are frustrating or bothering you, the smaller the issue it is to reconcile. The longer we put off things that need discussing, the more they grow in the dark. That said, it's also wise to spend a little time considering which battles to pick.

The foundational part of this daily connection is to lead with asking questions and listening. As mentioned before, asking questions helps you to not make assumptions about things, and then really listening for your person's point of view enables you to hear their thoughts, heart, and intentions. This goes a long way toward really understanding your spouse. When the majority of your communication is talking and not listening, then we will most often fail to connect and find solutions together.

The easiest way you can make this happen is to attach your time together to something you do each night. I found that when I got home before KC did (this was typical pre-kids,) I had a moment to change clothes, decompress, and transition into down time. Then, when he got home, I was ready to engage, but he needed a bit of time to transition. If forced to engage with me straight away without any transition time, he wasn't in the best mindset. Rightly so, he needed transition time from work to home, just as I did. Before you have kids, if you choose to have them, this is somewhat easier. Once kids come into the scenario, you'll need to define and agree on what those first few moments look like between arriving home and when full engagement happens. If you practice this before kids enter the family picture, this will just be a matter of adjusting roles until you can circle back to discuss your day. This takes teamwork, conversation, and lots of understanding.

Once we'd both transitioned to home life after work, we usually tried to exercise before the dinner routine. We might chat while we stretched, he might come hang out in the kitchen with me while I made dinner, or I'd go sit out on the porch while he barbecued. During this time we'd chat and share our days. This time was great for connecting as a couple, as best friends intentionally sharing their daily lives together. We cultivated our friendship by asking questions about one another's day, listening to each other, and sharing what was going on while we did the common activities couples do after work in the evenings.

Be Honest & Fight Fair

As you and your spouse collaborate on nonnegotiables for your own marriage, honesty must be a nonnegotiable. It might seem like a no-brainer, but verbally committing to one another that you will tell the truth is a critical component in a healthy marriage. Asking your spouse to always be truthful and being willing to speak truth in return—even with the hard truth topics—is an important part of building trust. That said, it takes maturity and sometimes courage to hear from your person when they are dissatisfied with an aspect of your relationship or the way things may be for a season. This is why it's important to learn to communicate with respect.

If you've been wounded in the past by someone who has spoken to you in an unkind or even critical way during an altercation, it can be scary to willingly expose yourself to your spouse's feedback. How conflict was handled in your family of origin will play a large role in your adult view of conflict if you haven't worked through or acknowledged your experience as an adult. If your spouse is uncomfortable or frustrated or dissatisfied with an aspect of your relationship or how you are doing something, it might be a trigger for you to retreat to what comes natural for you based on old patterns going all the way back to childhood. Patterns you might not even be aware of because they have become a part of your natural response. Let's be honest, in marriage we can get on one another's nerves. If we aren't careful, we can pop off with a short response or critical reply that can turn things south really quickly. This is why it's so important to know yourself well enough to help your spouse learn how to communicate with you in a way that's most productive, and vice versa.

Conflict resolution can be risky and can make one or both parties feel emotionally unsafe if we don't have our anger under control before we sit down to resolve an issue. Typically, KC gets more mad than I do emotionally, and he needs time to separate himself to sift through his thoughts so he can communicate with respect and a cool head. We've compromised to resolve issues in a manner that makes sense for both of us. He'll ask for space if he needs it, and I've learned to not dig in to settle it exactly when it works for me (typically immediately). What's worth noting here is that if he asks for space to cool off a little, then we've agreed that it's his responsibility to come back to me as soon as he's able to talk and resolve the matter at hand. He doesn't ask for time so he can stew, but rather for the purpose of doing a self-check for his attitude, heart, and mindset, so we can have resolution. He won't just leave an unsettled situation for hours or days. He's committed to not allowing himself to be stubborn. The goal in any disagreement is always to work it out to healthy, respectful resolution. KC says, "My parents approached every disagreement ready to fight to win to 'claim the hill.' I don't want to view a disagreement with Traci as a 'win-lose' thing, but to resolve it because she's my person, and even in a disagreement, I want the best for her."

Define early on what makes you feel safe, and what you're feeling in hard conversations. Discussing how conflict was handled in your home growing up will be good insight both for you and your spouse. Talk about and establish boundaries for conflict when you're not in conflict, so when the time comes for hard or eggshell topics to be discussed, you can start out approaching it from an informed place about how the other one best receives constructive feedback or even anger and frustration. It takes a lot of courage if you've been wounded before (and haven't we all been wounded in conflict with someone in our life?) to feel safe enough to welcome open and honest feedback that might be received as rejection or disappointment. Some of us would rather avoid conflict at all costs because our brains have catalogued any honest conversation that has potential for heat, frustration, or anger as scary, hurtful, or destructive. That's why the personality book and learning how to express love to your spouse in the best way that they receive it is so important for healthy conversations during conflict resolution.

If you haven't noticed, what I'm trying to show you is that conflict is a normal, typical part of living with another human being, especially in a marriage that goes the distance. What I want you to take away from this might surprise you: the most important part of conflict resolution is not the solution itself, but rather the process that you adopt as a couple to come to resolution with the end game in mind. Read that again. The point is not the individual issue at hand, but rather, acknowledging that what you want in the long run includes the other person, so this issue that you are currently discussing or working through at any time is just a place to practice using your new tools for conflict. You're fighting for something (your marriage) and against something (division), and you're on the same team. Instead of building a wall with stored "rocks" (grudges) that divide you, every resolved issue becomes building material for a foundation that supports and secures your marriage.

We chose three core intentions for our marriage: keeping our marriage the central relationship in our family; having regular, truthful, open communication; and fighting respectfully and fair. For us, our relationship with God would be the bedrock of our marriage, and these three would become the fundamental principles anchored to that foundation. Like you'll have, we had many, many other things we wanted to intentionally put into our marriage and family as well, but our mutual faith is a piece that cannot be left out, because for us, it was the belief behind the purpose in all of it. We desired for our faith in God to be played out to the best of our ability in the healthy relationships within the family. We wanted our children to see that our words and our actions were in alignment with what we professed to believe about God and about ourselves, and that our belief would serve as an example for healthy relationpships outside the home. What we learned from one another in the safety of home would better equip us for every other relationship that moved beyond the family. Things like:

- self-confidence
- understanding differences
- asking for forgiveness when you've messed up
- extending grace and forgiveness for wrongs done by others
- extending grace and forgiveness to yourself
- learning the vulnerability of trust
- finding confidence from those who love you unconditionally
- setting and keeping healthy boundaries
- discerning truths from untruths
- the value of hard work
- earning respect by being trustworthy

The list goes on and on for the benefits of creating a solid foundation rather than building a rock pile. One day when I am old and looking back at the end of our lives, I desire for KC and I to see a lifetime of rich, fulfilling relationships built in the daily conversations and cultivation of our relationship. I want that for you too. Knowing what I want at the end of my story helps me to not only make hard decisions in the moment, but to keep my eyes focused on something much bigger than myself when things get messy or when they don't seem to be working the way I'd hoped they would. The same goes for you.

We protect and intentionally layer these things into our lives knowing that many of them won't come to fruition for years, and that is something worth mentioning. Sure, we share pieces of our lives on social media because it's good to celebrate those beautiful moments, but it's just a small part of the much bigger picture. Those moments where it all comes together let us know that what we are doing is on track, and they are starting to take root in the relationship. But many times, it's messy, and it feels like we aren't making any progress. In fact, it would have never dawned on me to write this book even 15 years ago. Why? Because we were in the thick of it; the junior high and high school years with our older kids where at least one kid was coming off the rails at any given time. Back then I can remember KC and I working as hard as we ever have to stay connected, positive, and on the same team when our marriage was under the pressure of teenage years. Now on the other side of that season, I'm so thankful that we let those moments bring us together, rather than separate us.

For the sake of their privacy, my kids' stories are rarely shared by me, but the years when they were growing up were very trying years. This is why at the start of this book I recommend taking those tests to understand yourself and your spouse. Contrary to what you might believe, having children doesn't mean you give birth to, or adopt, a little mini-you. That's a whole other person: personality, love language, gifts, talents, strengths, and weaknesses all rolled into one little being for you to discover as you raise them up and help them become the best version of themselves over the course of about 20 years and beyond.

Part of collaborating with your spouse in how you'll go after what you really want in your relationships will involve each of your strengths and weaknesses being applied to the raising of each of the different little humans who might one day enter your family. As the saying goes, "Hold tightly to the mission and loosely to the methods." At all times KC and I had an overall mission that we were trying to accomplish as we created a culture in our marriage and eventually our family, but the method differed situationally. Sometimes the methods that worked six months prior no longer had the same impact. We regularly needed to recommit to the overall goal, as we collaborated on a new way. We'll get into that in the next chapter.

Key Choices

Grab your notebook for when you meet up with your spouse to discuss your action plan. You'll want to write down different ideas as you talk. If all of this is new for you, it might be hard at first. Just write down your thoughts as you go. No thought is too "out there." If you're looking for a quick read for some basic boundaries to set for your marriage relationship, I recommend the marriage booklet *A Good Beginning* by Peter L. Velander, M.S.

As you process how you want conflict to look like in your marriage, jot down and discuss what conflict resolution looked like in each of your families of origin as children. Write down what makes you feel comfortable and what makes you feel threatened or afraid.

Action Steps

1. As you make your list of nonnegotiables, you can divide your list into two lists. Or three. Or six. You can have as many as you like, but remember to keep it as simple as possible! You can make a list for your marriage, a list for your family, and a list for your professional relationships. Some lists will intersect, and that's absolutely normal and acceptable! Whether it's in your notes on your smart phone or on an actual paper notebook, make as many categories

as you'd like. A good rule of thumb is to ask, *Is this in line with our overall goal as a couple?*

2. Keep it simple! Start small and build on it. You have a lifetime to create your relationships, so don't overwhelm yourself with a hundred new things to start doing, or you won't do any. (Can you tell I'm speaking from experience?) Start, then course correct along the way.

3. As always, if you feel like you have some blocks that prevent you and your significant other from moving forward due to hurt or misunderstandings in the past, by all means find a mentor or counselor to help you get unblocked. Your relationship is far too important to not give your all toward moving forward, free of things holding you back. Stay positive! Don't allow yourself to get discouraged!

Chapter
5

Commit Consistently

*"Commitment is doing the thing you said you were going
to do long after the mood you said it in has left you."*
—Unknown

Committing to the process of the 5 Cs is the point when intention turns to action on a consistent basis. When KC and I made vows to one another we committed to three things. First, we individually committed to ourselves that we chose to be married, we chose to be married to each other, and we committed to all the known and unknown of being in a growing, monogamous marriage for life. We signed up for all of it. Our values and faith guided us as we chose one another not just on the big day in the dress & coattails, but for all the days of our merged lives. As people of faith, we committed to invite God into our marriage, believing him to be the creator of marriage (which also made marriage for us a spiritual convenant), and to do our best to keep God as the central member of the marriage. Each of us committed to invite his spirit to have full access to our hearts and mind to help us make wise decisions and to change us where and when necessary.

Second, we committed to doing what is right, as we understood it according to our beliefs about marriage. We committed to openness, honesty, faithfulness, truthfulness, the act of love, and showing up every day to make our marriage work and thrive. We committed to staying in the long conversations that were hard and to forgive one another when we were hurt and even before the other asked forgiveness.

We committed to continually choose to stay and work things through when leaving seemed easier or better because, deep down, we didn't really believe quitting is better.

Lastly, we committed to bring children into our family and in so doing, we committed to do everything within our power physically, mentally, and spiritually to love one another and keep the marriage together for life. We committed to keeping our family unit together for the betterment of our future children's spiritual, mental, and physical wellbeing.

You made commitments as well; have you thought about what they were, and what they mean to you lately? Creating a marriage that lasts requires living in a continual state of re-committing and buying in to the big picure, and because your relationship will never be perfect, it will always be in process on some level. There will always be some aspect of your relationship or situation that you wish were different. The art of the process is learning to discern which details require a closer look and which things you need to let go. A healthy marriage means we allow ourselves and the other person the space to grow into the people we've decided we want to be, and to give grace when there's a gap between that image and today. For example, while you might agree that you both want to have better communication than what was modeled for you when you were growing up, realistically it will require one, and likely both, of you to learn how to actually speak and listen differently. Committing to the process requires regularly recommitting to one another as you set your plan in motion.

> A healthy marriage means we allow ourselves and the other person the space to grow into the people we've decided we want to be.

While you may have agreed on many issues back when you were mapping out what you want your marriage and family to look like as you collaborated on your plans, staying committed to the execution of those plans is where the learning curve (challenge) will be. It sounds great to agree to speak more respectfully to one another, but learning how to hold your tongue or use more respectful, on-topic language in the heat of the moment will take time. To no longer give full vent to what so easily has come rolling out of your mouth for years takes not only a singular decision to behave differently moving forward, but the consistent action of following through after that decision is made. Especially when a disrespectful statement comes to mind in an argument. We've established that we must give ourselves the right balance of asking for and expecting more of ourselves and our spouse, but also forgiving with the understanding that it's really hard to undo a lifelong habit of wrong responses. To understand if it's going to take root, we must commit to the long game.

Take the Pulse on the Health of Your Marriage

When I was forty-five I started noticing some changes happening, physically. Assuming that what I was experiencing was a natural part of getting older, it didn't occur to me to see a doctor. I Googled a little, like many of us do, and basically found that while every body is different, my symptoms were pretty much in the normal range for my age. For safe measure, I asked a few ladies in my friend groups, women a few steps further along in life, and came up with pretty much the same answer as I'd found on Google, so I didn't do anything about it. What I was experiencing, I surmised, was part of the normal aging process, enduring the steps of getting closer to "the change" (menopause).

I did as much as I could to take care of myself, like exercising regularly and eating healthy, but when my annoying symptoms began interfering with life and business, I headed to my doctor. She ran bloodwork that didn't raise any flags, and gave me some things to try in the way of my nutrition and supplements, but as time went on, my symptoms continued and eventually got more disruptive. By the time my doctor ordered an ultrasound, I was forty-seven, and I don't think anyone was expecting them to find what they did: multiple non-cancerous tumors called fibroids in my uterus, and one was the size of a cantaloupe! While I was shocked, I felt very validated in how uncomfortable I had been feeling, and after KC and I made some decisions, shortly thereafter surgery was scheduled. I prepared by getting as physically fit as I could prior to surgery. My surgery was a success, recovery was slow but uncomplicated, and life moved forward. Now, those appointments and that process is all behind me, and I don't even think about it, but I learned many lessons on the journey and grew in the process of all of the waiting and testing. My faith and patience "muscles" were strengthened with each test, each step forward. After surgery, I learned how to live in a "new norm" as my body healed in the down time. And I now appreciate good health on the other side of that whole experience in a way I hadn't before. Hardship can make you so thankful if you allow it to.

I share this story because going through the processes of communicating in marriage is like that medical journey in a lot of ways. Both scenarios require patience as you go through the process of discovery, to identify the deeper, root issues that are causing the disruptive pain or discomfort that you're dealing with, while not expecting perfection or results immediately. But unlike a medical issue, where we can run tests and read x-rays, it takes time to dig down through emotions to identify the larger relational issue that's causing disruption. While we don't like it, we understand that it takes time and sometimes a lot of trials in the process of pinpointing and treating an illness in the body. The same is true when two people are working to identify and work through the intricacies of pain points in a marriage relationship. Oftentimes it's as simple as an issue of personality differences, but sometimes it's deeply rooted in a past wound or unhealthy belief or pattern that's deep inside, unaddressed (or perhaps tucked away intentionally) until it was triggered in the intimacy of a marriage relationship.

Just like we'd fight like crazy against a tumor or cancer in our body, shouldn't we fight just as hard against a "cancer" (division) in our marriage? My heart grieves for what might have been in relationships that have broken off, if only those involved had a perspective shift and tools to use to fight for their spouse instead of against him/her. There are many different reasons why marriages have broken up; we all bring wounds from other relationships into the marriage, either from what we've seen in our parents or in our own personal relationship history. Relationships starting out with protective walls up won't fully allow either person to engage on the level that a healthy marriage requires. Though not a helpful mindset to enter into a lifelong commitment, I can understand how scary that would be, especially if you've been wounded in the past. It takes time to learn to trust and allow yourself to be known, but what greater relationship to be vulnerable in than your marriage?

On the opposite end of the spectrum are those who enter into marriage with a somewhat lackadaisical attitude. Give it a try, and if it gets too hard or you happen to grow in another direction from your spouse, then divorce is always there as an option to walk away and try again. But with that mindset, wouldn't you eventually outgrow the next person? Of course, you're going to change! Can you imagine how sad it would be if you didn't grow leaps and bounds, even from age twenty to age thirty? In my fifty-one years of living so far, I have not seen any married couples who have grown together by accident; it takes a lifetime of intentionally connecting and recommitting over and over to your person as they too grow, at their own pace. That is the most amazing thing about marriage; when you both do the work, when you both regularly "re-up" on your initial promise and do so for a lifetime, your growth spurs on the growth of your spouse, and vice versa. Part of living in a marriage for life is that you learn to stay in the discomfort between the "now" and the "not yet." Knowing that it takes a lifetime of changing and growing into the next best versions of ourselves, continually choosing to love the person we promised to love through it all—that's commitment.

> When you both do the work, when you both "re-up" on your initial promise and do so for a lifetime, your growth spurs on the growth of your spouse, and vice versa.

Commit to the Long Game

"Life is what happens when you've got something else planned." My mom has said that more times than I can count. Our commitment is strengthened every time we choose to fully engage and address issues in our marriage in the midst of a busy life, in the times when we aren't sure how to handle the situation, or when it's just plain exhausting to engage and work it through to resolution. I heard a marriage and family therapist once say that, all too often, married couples who come into his office have waited three years too long to get help. He didn't say too late, but too long. The issues are bigger than they needed to be had they asked for tools and help sooner. Maybe regular conversation isn't happening as often as you'd like because one of you has been working longer hours or traveling more than normal for a season. Perhaps if you have kids, the baby has not been sleeping on schedule, or a sports season has you passing one another taking kids to and from their practices with not a lot of time to connect. This is on some level unavoidable, as life is full; but we must be intentional to stay connected. Sometimes, for short seasons, it's impractical for time purposes to deal with the issue at hand because some seasons are just busier than others. I don't recommend this often, but sometimes you just have to put a pin in it until you can give it the time it needs, committing to address it as soon as the schedule allows. Don't allow yourself to grow cold to your spouse in the wait time.

If an issue goes unresolved too long in a marriage, one or both people can feel very disconnected surprisingly quickly. A marriage is like a living, breathing organism that requires daily attention for it to grow healthily. If issues are left unresolved or unaddressed for too long, our response to one another can run the gamut of negative emotions as the relationship feels the impact. As in health matters, if we leave something unaddressed for a long period of time, it gets worse, not better. Psychologist Les Parrott says, "Buried feelings have a high rate of resurrection."[16]

Typically, by the time an unaddressed issue in a marriage comes to a head it's a full-on blow up. It can get ugly fast and quickly become a big, emotional explosion with both sides not only addressing the original issue, but digging into their rock piles of stored up, unresolved past issues. Throwing big and little "rocks" as hard and fast as they can in the form of angry, hurtful words. Whatever it started out to be can go downhill quickly when it's combined with negative self-talk ("I know what s/he really means by that"; "It's what s/he always does"; "S/he never thinks of my feelings"; "This will never get better"; "Does he even love me?" The list goes on). Negative, assumptive fighting language doesn't help this either.

When we internalize our negative feelings toward our spouse, and don't have open, healthy, respectful communication (even if heated) the other person doesn't have a chance to speak to those negative thoughts to agree with or dispute them. Negative internal self-talk produces an emotional response as we believe what we've assumed is the truth. Before we know it, by the time we sit down to talk, we have an open-and-shut case built against our person, and they haven't had a chance to speak to it. This is the danger of ignoring something in the hopes that it will go away. When we commit to the habit of addressing issues of conflict regularly, our relationship begins to live in a healthy environment of consistent, open communication. When our marriage is healthy, the relationship has the capacity to grow and thrive.

Just as a tumor grows when ignored or untreated, so can anger, bitterness, and emotional wounds that are left unaddressed in a person. In the physical body, the treatment can take longer because it's grown into something bigger and harder to remove. Though we want to rush the process through the variety of bloodwork, tests, and x-rays, we understand that when our body has something wrong with it, it will take time to figure out the best treatment plan. Interestingly, we don't have the same mindset about emotional wounds. A growing, healthy relationship with regular, respectful, air-clearing conversation takes time to cultivate, especially if we start out with a little (or big) rock pile built against the other person and a history of approaching conflict with unhealthy and unproductive problem-solving skills. Every unkind or disrespectful word spoken, every time your hurt feelings in the past went unaddressed can grow with negative power in your memory. Even more so if you emotionally visit those wounds. Maybe you tried in the past to bring it up, and you didn't find the healing or apology you wanted, so you're resolved to not go there again for fear of getting dismissed or chastised. Conflict resolution takes time to navigate, which calls on us to regularly commit to that process. It takes courage and patience and kindness to continue to work on your marriage by opening yourself up regularly to someone who you don't fully understand yet, or maybe before you fully understand yourself. But just like every blood test gives more information about the physical body to the doctor, every conversation serves as an indicator of where the other person is coming from.

I had a dear friend who had been married for several years and who had raised three wonderful children through to young adulthood. After nearly two decades of marriage, the issues that had been ignored for years surfaced, demanding, at last, to be addressed. By the time she came for mentoring to discuss healthy communication, both she and her husband were basically living separate lives and had more than a decade of of stored-up issues; a huge rock pile. We began a process of digging down to see if we could address not just the "little rocks" on top (the most recent, annoying issues that were small but served as a tipping point), but instead to identify the patterns and underlying core issues. We didn't spend a lot of time addressing those little things that felt bigger than they were, which for her felt like evidence of "just one more example" that the relationship was lacking. By that point, even the smallest disagreements felt big, but that's because they were piled on top of years' worth of unaddressed wounds, offenses, let downs, and misunderstandings that had been swept under the rug for the sake of maintaining peace in their fast-paced life. This had instead, created the opposite. They made their commitment back on the big day in the dress, but somehow, over time, she and her husband's marriage had slowly eroded into roommate and co-parent status. Neither were happy about it, but after years of not communicating, neither one knew how to change it.

As she and I began to unpack the details and patterns for the sake of charting a new way, our goal was not to look at each and every painful memory (though many were amazingly stored in her brain like hash marks keeping invisible score). We started by taking a look at her and her husband's individual makeup. We looked at how each of them were wired, just as we did in Chapter One, identifying their individual personalities and love languages. Then, we looked at themes in their conflicts. It's always amazing to me how simplified a decade worth of wounds from poor communication can be when you look at how the individual is wired to approach an issue as compared to their partner, as well as how each views the way love is communicated. If you take two people who have lived together for any amount of time, but don't understand how their styles of handling conflict interact with each other, or how one person expresses or receives love from the other, there is going to be miscommunication and misunderstanding. In so many relationships, just learning about yourself and coming into agreement with how your spouse is wired to communicate and receive information opens up a new understanding of how to move forward with healthy communication together.

Not surprisingly, as my friend and I began to talk, we quickly discovered that the surface issues were not the problem. The pattern of poor communication rooted in misunderstanding one another for years had been compounded by covering up that dissatisfaction with busyness. They both did what comes so easily for married people who are moms and dads: they poured all of their focus into their kids and into their work. They operated like work partners and slowly let the marriage relationship cool to the point where both were no longer angry; they'd just grown into two fully functioning people, married, but isolated from one another. When pressed, they each said privately, "We grew apart."

While this is true to some degree, it certainly doesn't have to be the death sentence so many believe it to be. Yes, time did pass. Yes, they did grow older. They experienced life for months and years in the same house, in the same family, but without checking in on all of the small and large issues along the way. Their marriage operated dysfunctionally, even as other areas of their personal lives may have thrived. But their personal growth stalled in a part of each of them, hung up on areas not worked through in their marriage. That part remained undeveloped. The marriage just sort of sat there in the background of the busyness of life, waiting to be addressed in a healthy way in order to develop and move forward.

At any time, when both people choose to reconnect and work again on the areas they have been sidelining for a season, no matter how uncomfortable it is at first, they can grow together again. It's entirely possible. I know because I've seen it happen in other people, and I've certainly seen it to a smaller degree in my own marriage, where two people learn to grow through a challenging season rather than quit and start over. When KC and I talk with someone in this place, we point them back to remembering all of the reasons why they fell in love and made the commitment to begin with.

Every relationship gets to a point where one or the other (or both) could give up because they hit that spot that needs to be addressed. I'm telling you, if you give up with one person, you may be surprised to find that a similar issue in the next relationship will eventually come up. The unfortunate thing about quitting or throwing in the towel rather than working through an issue is that you'll end up dragging the undeveloped part in you right up to that same moment in the next relationship. Every relationship takes work. Why not learn all the lessons as you develop one relationship that goes the distance, rather than move from one to the next? Of course, in some relationships one might be all in, and the other just won't engage. These five tools for designing a relationship with healthy communication are for both people to engage with. A growing relationship takes two. Sure, one can take the lead at different times, but for a relationship to grow and survive, it takes two to engage. Sometimes, one of you has to be the strong one of the two for a season if one is struggling more than the other; that happens in most marriages. But eventually you get to a point where you are at the end of what you can carry alone in a marriage.

That happened in our marriage. KC never intentionally disconnected. He struggled with undiagnosed seasonal depression. It wasn't talked about much back then, but we saw the effects up close and personal each year as the long, cheery, bright summer days gave way to the cooler, shorter days of fall. To his credit, he really did engage as much as he was able with what he knew. But without intending to, as the season changed, he went inward, quiet, and somewhat emotionally inaccessible. Because it was seasonal, he would eventually emerge from what we perceived as his "funk" and because life was busy and we had a bunch of kids to distract me, it would get back to normal between us. We tried to discuss it, but he truly didn't know what was going on inside of him. It was a lonely time of year for me, one where I was left feeling disconnected and confused as to what was happening. After a few years, and with the invention of the internet, I started researching his symptoms online. It was a process of discovery for both of us: an unseen illness that showed up in the form of emotional disconnect every year. It wore on me in particular, and eventually, I got to the end of my ability to rally and carry it alone and waived a flag of surrender. That was a defining moment for us. It's a scary thing to say, "I can't do this alone anymore. I'm at the end of me and what I can do alone." Asking your partner to engage on a deeper level when perhaps they feel like they don't know how really is laying it all on the line; but sometimes situations become drastic (not dramatic, there's a difference), and we have to say some extremely difficult, transparent things with loving humility, inviting the other person to engage and fight with you for your marriage. I had given everything I had, and I needed him to engage in a new way. I didn't want to manipulate him with my words, but to truly show him that I loved him and needed my partner.

I asked KC just last week if he could remember back to what he was thinking when we sat in our living room having that discussion. Did he remember what was it that made this conversation different, what caused him to hear what I said in a new way? How did he sense this was a defining moment? He said, "I was at the end of me too. I could hear something different in your voice, and I knew I needed to do something. I also knew that it had to be for the right reasons. I couldn't change just for you. If I had, it would have been like painting an old, beat-up house. I needed to do it for me, to become better than I was. I needed to build a whole new house." Rather than trying to conjure up the strength and emotional courage to make something happen just for the appearance of results, he deeply desired to grow to the next best version of himself. Growing for the right reasons would serve him well and serve our marriage well. When we show up in our relationships as our best selves for the right reasons, everyone benefits.

I am forever grateful that KC didn't get defensive (he could have; those are scary words to hear, I'm sure). I'm thankful that he really heard my heart, and that he said, "OK. I hear you. I will do my best." He did so by picking up a book titled *Feeling Good* by Dr. David D. Burns, M.D. A book that radically changed his life, my life, our marriage, and the way he showed up in our family. This book had been given to him a couple months before and was sitting on his bedside table. After our conversation, he walked back to our room, picked it up, and read for the next couple of hours. That book was an amazing catalyst that started him on the road to changing habitual negative thought habits.

I'm not implying that the book is the answer for every person who struggles with anxiety or depression, but the book addresses habits for how one might respond to negative thoughts and how they affect depressive feelings. Here is a little excerpt from the book that changed KC's life, and consequently, our marriage, for the better.

> [Y]our thoughts create your feelings. The powerful principle at the heart of cognitive therapy is that your feelings result from the messages you give yourself. In fact, your thoughts often have much more to do with how you feel than what is actually happening in your life.

This isn't a new idea. Nearly two thousand years ago the Greek philosopher, Epictetus, stated that people are disturbed "not by things, but by the views we take of them." In the Book of Proverbs (23:7) in the Old Testament you can find this passage: "For as he thinks within himself, so he is." And even Shakespeare expressed a similar idea when he said: "For there is nothing either good or bad, but thinking makes it so." (Hamlet, Act 2, Scene 2)[17]

Through this book, KC discovered that so much of how he felt in that change of seasons each year was a result of a lifetime habit of allowing a series of negative thoughts to take him down a slippery slope, leading to crippling, isolating, hopeless depression in many instances. For him, this discovery was freeing because it taught him how to recognize negative thoughts, redirect them, and enable him to take back his emotional responses. For me, this discovery was freeing because the book gave him new tools, and he began to transform as soon as he put them into practice. I was so thankful that he was willing to do the hard work to retrain his thinking. For whatever reason, that day my words woke him out of a foggy "this is just the way it is" existence, and he chose to engage and willingly fight for his own happiness, and ultimately for our marriage. As he immediately went to work to "build a new house," our relationship grew like it was on vitamins.

I believe that the reason we could immediately begin to grow together was because we leaned heavily into our faith in God and invited Him to be an active partner in our marriage. I don't mean to make this an uncomfortable moment if you haven't invited God to be a part of your life or marriage, but I would be leaving out the true "all star" in our marriage if I gave all the credit to that book alone. I'm aware that faith-based marriages end, but I don't believe that means

God helps some and doesn't help others. We both are responsible to do all we can to honor our commitment. We were two people who truly were willing to invite God's spirit into our interaction, thought processes, and behaviors. We were willing to do the work to stay and to allow Him to lead us. We both chose to keep our hearts pliable, to stay humble, and to be teachable. We regularly chose to be willing to do the right thing when the old habits came far more naturally and easily. I strongly believe that the God who brings two people together for life through marriage also enables those willing partners to keep that commitment.

Practically, it was a huge benefit that we'd been trying all along to keep our rock pile addressed regularly. As soon as KC started taking steps to reroute some of his lifelong depression-creating thought patterns, he didn't emerge to find me ready to address a rockpile of stored-up wounds. To the best of our ability, we'd kept our conflicts dealt with, and our slate was pretty clean. He'd been sidelined with an unseen illness we were unaware of and was now getting tools, and I was getting a new and improved version of my man.

Only the people in the marriage know the intricate details of their relationship, and while I am a proponent of creating an intentionally beautiful marriage for life, I also know that not all marriages will go the distance. If one person isn't sure that they want to commit to stay and fight, it gets complicated, and the marriage is more fragile. These 5 Cs can help a couple intentionally create the kind of marriage they desire by navigating common sticking points and helping them find their way on their chosen course, even through the really hard times that happen with any couple who goes the lifelong distance. You, and only you, get to decide if you are a couple who wants to commit to staying through the hard times and creating something amazing over a lifetime. What I don't want to do is make a reader feel bad because the details of their marriage were beyond the 5 C process; maybe in order for them to move forward it was best to go two different paths. No, I want to help you identify how to use these tools to work toward something that is bigger than you and how to move back and forth through the 5 Cs for a lifetime in both big and small issues. If you have tried, maybe gotten counseling, and your relationship ended either with or without your permission because it had become toxic and/or beyond repair, never lean into shame. It's hard enough to deal with the loss, disappointment, and even regret, but shame has no part in healthy healing. Looking at the situation and owning your part for the sake of healing, yes; but shaming, whether internally or from an external source, serves no purpose. The truth is, many of life's lessons come out of our pain. Pain births lessons we never would choose if given the choice but are ours nonetheless to mine for the beauty that comes from ashes. If you have an ended marriage in your past, healing and recovery is found in the process of grieving the loss and preparing for something new. The lessons are found in that tension of addressing what you might have done differently, owning your part, and moving forward with new tools so you don't repeat old behaviors that didn't serve you or your previous marriage. My prayer is that these tools set you up to learn how to use healthy communication in your relationships from this day forward. Not perfect, but healthier.

I was at a work event earlier this year when a friend approached me to catch up. In the last several years since I'd known her, she had gone through a hard divorce and had recently remarried. I was asking how things were, and she was just bubbling with excitement to be in a healthy relationship that was based on mutual respect and where both partners were fully engaged in growing together. She said, "Traci, I know you're all about marriage for life, and I am too; but sometimes it just doesn't work out the way we'd like. I tried for so long to carry it alone, and in the end, I was the only one trying to save it. The contrast from that marriage to this one is night and day! I can tell you that my husband and I will stay married for life. It's so nice to be in a marriage where we both are engaged! I'm so happy!"

For years, my friend had battled alone for her marriage, but in the end her husband was unwilling to engage and fight for their relationship. I do believe in marriage for life and that when you stand and make that lifelong promise you're saying "yes" to all of it; but one person cannot make another person follow through on the promise. Somewhere along the line for his own reasons, her husband gave up trying. I have no idea what his background and circumstances were, but when you have one spouse committed to the process of growing together and getting counseling if necessary, and the other chooses to disengage, divorce sometimes happens. It makes me sad, for both her and him. He had a great woman, and when he was still in the position to turn it around, he didn't choose to engage to work things through. It breaks my heart, but I also know it happens in an imperfect world. Life is messy, and every marriage is really hard at times. That's a given. But we have choices. We get to commit every day to do all we can to make our marriage go the distance, so we are still standing together when we're old and gray.

Commit to Forgiving

Forgiveness is where many marriages either derail or level up. I think it's important to note that neither great marriages nor bad marriages happen as a result of a single event or day. It's a series of choices and discussions over time in support of a chosen outcome. The alternative is to just respond to life as it comes without a plan to create something on purpose, and that's usually when things go way off target. The "process" that happens in a long-term marriage where both partners have intentionally chosen to create something worth fighting for is different for every couple. I have not met one long-term married couple that has never had the opportunity or desire to throw in the towel at least once when it got hard. Knowing that it's a process and not expecting too much too soon allows us to mentally settle in to the safety of finding your way as a couple. Staying married for life requires committing to regularly extend forgiveness. A lot of forgiveness. To yourself and to your spouse.

Committing to the long game means settling in mentally and not expecting a complete makeover all at once in the areas that are difficult. It will take a lifetime to create your best version of yourself, and the same goes for your spouse. Your commitment will be tested in the day-to-day living and will also be where growth happens if you choose to let it. Your growth is completely within your own choices: in what you read, in what you do, in what you say, in how you say it. The person you will become, that older version of you sitting on that porch out in the future, is your choice now. This is where everything you have chosen, communicated, and collaborated about is lived out. It's where perseverance is created, and where you each set your mind to living in such a way that you make happen what you want for your life, marriage, and family. Putting it on paper and agreeing to commit consistently to trying new ways of responding and reacting will be critical to change actually happening. The reality is, it takes years of working to "win the day," day in and day out, for as long as you both shall live. It will get hard, and you'll have seasons when you'll see no progress, or even regression. Some days it might not feel like you won the day at all. Don't overemphasize the terrible days, because we all have them. Commit to giving your all in the now, and when your spouse is struggling, give him/her the grace to have a bad day too. Commit to stay and give your all in all seasons of life: where there is growth and where growth lies seemingly dormant, when you feel madly in love with your person and when your emotions are flatlined.

You will live in the process, because we are all in process until we breathe our last. Remind yourself that what you work for and create with intention is your legacy.

Plan to freely give grace and be patient when your spouse is working on making changes. Remember how hard it is to change an old habit in yourself. One habit. It takes time, patience, forgiveness, lots of conversations, and celebrating when things work. As with anything, committing to the process of a plan that serves your marriage and family well is the only way to achieve something amazing. Adjusting as life changes and the plan no longer fits will take intention, as well as a desire for something bigger and better long-term than what you're experiencing in the present. This is true of so many moments that happened in our marriage that it's almost hard to pick just one to share with you. But here's one.

One of the things KC and I decided to work on was a communication style that kept us both engaged. We communicate in two different ways. I prefer a back-and-forth conversation, where we popcorn thoughts back and forth, almost interrupting one another to finish the sentence and add on. KC prefers to gather his thoughts and share, uninterrupted, until his thought is finished and then have me respond (think presidential debate style). I cannot tell you how often I shut him down by my way of conversation. What I view as back-and-forth interaction, he views as me interrupting to agree, disagree, or clarify. I'd break in to say something, he'd lose his train of thought, and then he'd be frustrated because he lost the thought and couldn't bring it back easily. This is a classic example of wanting something (to have regular, good conversation in the middle of a busy life), communicating it clearly to one another, collaborating on the plan (him sitting with me in the kitchen after work while I finish up dinner), then letting it play out (committing to the process). We found that our conversation styles were missing the target with one another. Either of us may have been tempted after our first or fifth or sixth frustrating attempt at it to throw in the towel. Thankfully, we didn't. But it was a heck of a lot easier to *say* we were going to do something that sounds so healthy and normal, than to actually take a shot at it and end up frustrated because it wasn't intuitive, and it took work!

Honestly, this has been something that I have slowly gotten better at but still don't feel like I nail it. It's not because I don't value his way of communicating, but it just doesn't make sense to me and is counter to how I converse with other people. My perspective is that as he shares his thoughts in one uninterrupted "monologue," as I jokingly call it, there might be three or eight things in the middle that I want to address or have clarified or ask more questions about.

> Sometimes we need to discuss the PROCESS of discussing something in addition to what we're actually discussing!

By the time he's done, I might not remember all of the things I wanted to respond to. This is the reality of the process. Sometimes we need to discuss the process of discussing something in addition to what we're actually discussing!

Our commitment to the process means we both work on ourselves and are patient as progress is being made, however small, to allow one another the space to grow. Today, I might not wait until he's expressed every thought in his head on the topic, but I won't interrupt (much) either. I might slightly raise my hand to say, "May I add something here before you go on?" And that gives him the opportunity to say, "Let me finish this thought, and then you can jump in," or "Sure, I was done with my thought." I had to learn that he wasn't trying to be a "control freak" to get it all out in one breath without me interrupting, but that for his personal style of communicating, his brain loses the thought if he is interrupted. He had to learn that I wasn't being intentionally rude or disrespectful if I cut in to add on to what he was trying to articulate. Sometimes afterwards, we hug or congratulate ourselves on how well we worked through something so fast and painlessly, taking time to notice and address that we are making progress. And as often as possible, we verbalize our commitment to go the distance with one another so the other person has no doubts as to whether we are both *all in* for the long game.

Concentrate on Love

When we got married, the videographer went around to people at our wedding reception and asked them to speak into the camera and give us words of wisdom. One of the guests said, "Just always concentrate on love." To be honest, we laughed at that one as we watched because we thought, "That's a no-brainer!" We thought surely this person got a little camera shy and said something off the cuff that didn't land as intended. The truth is, she was spot-on. It was simple, wise advice, as we've come to discover after more than three decades of marriage. Taking one another for granted is such an easy thing to do. We get busy with life, we have to pay the bills, the car breaks down, one person works overtime, the other might be out of work for a time, the baby's sick, no one's sleeping well, the dog chewed up yet another shoe, our teenager is pressing all of our buttons; you name it, life has plenty of complications. That's true for everyone. And as life presses in, we go into protection mode, work mode, survival mode. Stress sets in and we can lose track of our most treasured relationships very quickly.

One of the things I consistently do is remind myself of all the things I love, admire, and respect about KC. I consciously keep my positive thoughts about him at the forefront of my mind. This has gotten easy now that I've done this exercise regularly for more than thirty years. It helps me to be less upset when little annoying things spring up, because I have chosen to be mindful about why

I love him. When I choose to remember why I love him on a regular basis, the annoying disagreements don't hold as much weight against that. When I remember all of the great attributes that KC has and why I'm drawn to him, it's very easy for me to do something nice for him. And when I do something nice for KC because I'm being mindful of how valuable he is to me, he notices, feels seen and loved, and because he is consciously remembering the things he loves and respects about me, he in turn stays soft-hearted toward me.

Now, it's not like we just sit and think of one another all day, every day. We have full-time jobs and home-life responsibilities on our plates as well. Distractions surround us, but we are intentional to make little "touches" during the day: a text, a phone call, sometimes having lunch together. In the middle of our busy days we intentionally take a moment to think on the other with gratitude, so our hearts regularly stay softened to the other. This way, we anticipate the evenings when we are around each other after work, and we get along like two people who really care about one another. Those little thoughts are like watering and putting nutrients into the soil of a plant. They grow our love when we are away, so that when we are together we are growing toward one another at a healthy rate.

Like many people in our nearly post-pandemic world, KC now works from home. However, for most of our marriage when he worked outside of the home and before cell phones, he'd leave me a note every morning, because he got up and left for work before I was awake. (LA traffic meant he had to leave very early.) From the time we were first married, every day I woke up to a note, scribbled on a notepad or on the back of an envelope. His little handwritten note every morning was a ritual that connected us from the first few minutes we were both awake. Today, it's an established tradition. When we got cell phones, he started sending me a text every morning, and oftentimes several times throughout the day. Just little touches that kept us in the forefront of one another's minds. When I started traveling for work, I began leaving him a little note tucked in our bed on his pillow. Again, this let him know that he's mine and I'm his, and that I love and value him so much even as the miles stretch between us. He's the kind of guy who loves to do home projects, so he began doing a surprise house project when I was away on business. I would come home to a fun new addition to our home or a finished project that we'd put off for a long time. He'd get the kids involved; maybe they'd install a ceiling fan, plant flowers in the garden, clean out a drain that had been backed up, or fix something that had been broken . . . it didn't have to be something big, but the kind of thing that really mattered to us because it was our home. Then, on the nights I'd arrive home, he'd cook me a hot, "welcome home" dinner with the kids. We called it "Dad's Chili," complete with corn bread or garlic bread and salad. I'd come home to a clean house, a hot meal, and a surprise project done! Can you tell his love language is acts of service? He didn't have to do those things, but he showed me that I mattered to him, and got the kids involved as well, which showed them how parents love each other and do nice things for one another. I'd often come home to a homemade "welcome home" sign on the door, and we'd have a nice family dinner together, happy to be reunited.

That's a beautiful portrait of a loving couple, isn't it? Now, I'll show you the underbelly yet still truthful side of that. I'm embarrassed to say that it took me a long time to fully understand his love language. Oh, I appreciated the projects and the clean house and hot meal, don't get me wrong! But my love languages are words of affirmation and physical touch. If I'm raw and honest, I would have loved a big expressive welcome home! For him to stop what he's doing as I walked through the door, hug me tight, and tell me all the ways he missed me and how glad he was that I was home. How it *actually* played out is that when I walked through the front door, he would look up from the chili pot, give me a sweet smile, and say, "Welcome home, babe!" No hooting, no hollering, no spinning me around as he kissed my face. I was the one who walked over to give him a big hug and kiss, where he'd say something like, "Oh, watch the stove, it's hot!" as he gave me a side hug back while still stirring.

In the old days the first thing I'd say was, "What's wrong?"

To which he'd reply, "Nothing, why?"

"Well, it's just that you don't seem happy to see me."

"What? You just walked through the door. I haven't had a chance to even say three words to you!"

It's embarrassing to open that up to the world, but I think you might be able to see it more clearly in my relationship than you may be able to see those "misses" in your own relationship. I felt immediately sad because his physical response to me wasn't what I would have ideally liked, so I incorrectly assumed that something might be wrong. He felt bad because he'd done all these things for me, and the first thing out of my mouth was, "What's wrong?" Our first evening home together for the first three-ish years of my traveling always went crooked in those first few minutes. We hadn't yet read the love languages book. We didn't know that we were both loving one another in the most expressive way we could. And though we were loving one another wholly, we were both left feeling somewhat misunderstood and sometimes unloved and unappreciated to some degree. Our huge breakthrough came when we realized through reading *The 5 Love Languages* that we were talking two different languages. His home project, clean house, and hot dinner was his way of picking me up, swinging me around, and kissing me passionately!

It takes time to learn a new language, and learning a love language is no different. KC now tries hard to be expressive verbally and physically with me, and I try to remember to do more things for him in the way of acts of service. Both of those do not come easily for either one of us, but if we had quit on one another in search of someone who spoke our language, I can guarantee that there would be some other gap in another part of a new relationship. Because everything we want from this life includes us staying together and in love, we learned a new language. His language is hard for me. I'm not naturally a servant in the area that he appreciates. Part of my process is to ask him for some ideas of things that I could do for him that would make him feel loved by me, and then make an effort to do them regularly. As odd as it might feel, telling him things that I would love for him to do and say (like hugging me tight and telling me he missed me while I was gone) allows him to make it a priority to do those things for me. Learning a different language for the sake of communicating to one another how much we love each other, so they really feel it, is important in marriage.

Sometimes, when life is busy, it's very easy to get out of the habit of practicing our new language, deferring to expressing ourselves naturally rather than what we choose intentionally. The same will happen for our spouse. That's when we have to be humble and bold enough to ask for what we need in a nonaggressive way. "Babe, I feel like we're talking two languages again, and it's feeling a little lonely. Can we make an effort, or maybe pick up that book again to do a little reviewing?" That's the gist of what we say, but we don't say it exactly like that. We talk to one another in a silly, playful way, expressing what we want, but not like we're reading a script. Make the language your own. This is your private relationship. Talk like you talk in private, but make sure you express yourself in a safe and loving way. No one has a meaningful heart change when they get snapped at or accused. Marriage isn't about getting your way. It's about finding your way. Together.

> Marriage isn't about getting your way. It's about finding your way. Together.

Be A Safe Person

Have you ever considered whether you are pereceived as a safe person in conflict and conversation? I didn't realize it, but I learned that I wasn't always giving a facial expression that showed myself as emotionally safe when I was upset. I was challenged once to ask those closest to me, "What's it like to be on the other side of me?" It was an exercise meant to reveal blind spots about myself and my relationships, and I was excited to do the exercise. I started with my own adult kids. Not having any idea of what they would say, I opened the conversation with, "What is something you experience with me that I might not know?" They were quick to respond.

"When you get mad, you get this look on your face that looks *really* mad. Your nostrils sorta flare, and when we were kids, we knew we were in trouble." I literally had no clue. I mean, I knew that I wanted them to know I was upset, so I meant to have a stern look on my face, but I didn't know I looked scary!

I went to the bathroom and without looking at the mirror, I tried to conjure up "the face." I thought of something that might make me mad as a mom. I thought of kids being unkind to one another, talking disrespectfully to me, or maybe lying about something, and I made the face as best as I could by memory of how I feel when I'm mad. Then I looked in the mirror. Yikes. They were right. It was an intimidating, almost mean facial expression. I'd never seen it before when just looking at myself in the mirror. It was a blind spot that I would never have known if I hadn't asked.

They were adults when I asked, so they were able to laugh and go easy on me. "To be fair, Mom, we were sometimes brats to each other and to you at times. You had a reason to be mad." Oh, the kindness of adult kids. But it got me thinking: I recognized how that face felt when I made it. At the time they told me, I was still in the habit of making that face when I would get upset. I knew that I made that face with KC when

I was angry. I realized that while I had been very intentional to choose non-accusing words in conversations of conflict, I hadn't monitored my facial expressions. Because people are visual, both my kids and KC saw my face before they heard my words, and that was sending a message that I never intended to send: prepare for battle. When I feel like someone is challenging me offensively, it is very hard to hear the message the other person is speaking because I mentally begin preparing my defense. Call it self-preservation or pride, but I intuitively start listening defensively, not with an openness to learn. It was difficult to learn that I was triggering that response in those closest to me, and definitely put me on the path to learning and practicing how to keep my face, voice tone, and words safe for the person I was communicating with.

What about you? What kind of environment is conducive to your learning? Do you do well with someone barking at you, or giving you the silent treatment? What about your spouse? Does an antagonistic environment open him/her up to really hear what you're saying? Probably not. Committing to create safe, healthy communication requires us to not just do or say whatever floats across our minds or emotions in the moment. It offers us an opportunity to choose our words wisely and respectfully in such a way that the other person feels safe to hear you, and to hear what you're actually saying. In order to have a productive conversation, it's our responsibility to communicate in such a way that our spouse can truly hear the message being delivered in such a loving (though possibly upsetting) space that it draws a healthy response from them. While it's true that you aren't responsible for the way your spouse responds, if you're truly honest with yourself, could you maybe deliver your message in a less conflict-inducing way? Did you possibly end the conversation at the start by jumping down their throat, or maybe even assuming some things that s/he meant, and responding to your assumption, rather than asking clarifying questions to see where s/he is really at?

Or perhaps you have been so concerned about not hurting your spouse or don't like muddying the waters that somewhere along the line you began the unhealthy habit of pushing down offenses so as not to rock the boat. Both cause division, and whether you land in one camp or the other, you can commit today to the process of learning a new way of healthy communication to show that conflict resolution can be safe and productive.

> Commitment is doing the thing you said you were going to do long after the mood you said it in has left you.

There are no words to describe how powerful your commitment to one another grows with every rock pile you commit to diminish together, turning each resolved issue into a rock solid foundation of healing and releasing. Commitment is forgiving one another, concentrating on why you love each other, and being emotionally safe to grow with one another. Commitment is doing the thing you said you were going to do long after the mood you said it in has left you. The process takes work, and it is worth it.

Key Choices

Have you ever attended a marriage conference? These are typically a good place to go to brush up on some of the areas you may be lacking in. If you're thriving, it's a good place to learn tools for how to make your marriage even better! You can ask your pastor or clergy if you attend a church, but a Marriage Builders conference or seminar will provide tools and tips for keeping your marriage thriving. As with anything involving relationships, it's always good to stay with the basics as you grow. Author and speaker Gary Chapman also hosts *The 5 Love Language* seminars for people who want to meet one another's emotional needs. Whatever you feel would meet your current need, sign up and go; you won't be sorry!

Action Steps

1. Every week set a time to regularly communicate, apart from other people, and with cell phones off or put away. Protect your time together as you keep your intimate, honest, regular communication open and flowing. Again and again verbalize your commitment to your person, your marriage, and to healthy new patterns and to fight *with* your spouse *for* your marriage . . . for life. Ask your person what it's like to experience you in times of conflict, and how you can be an emotionally safer person for them to communicate with.

2. Try new things together! A couple who plays together has more fun as they stay together! Take a dancing class, buy bikes and ride along the ocean or lakeside, join a bowling league, go see a play, visit a museum, learn to cook together, take an art class, garden together, walk the dog. Don't let time pass without intentionally taking time to learn something fun and new together!

3. As you grow and your marriage expands, don't allow anyone to come between you and your spouse; not your parents, not your in-laws, not your friends, and not even your kids. Your marriage covenant is between you, your spouse, and God. Every other relationship you have will only be enhanced when your marriage is healthy, thriving, and protected as your most valued earthly relationship. Your children will blossom and launch when their parents love and respect one another. Remember this: should you have them, you want your children to grow up and create their own adventure-filled lives by launching to life outside your home. But your spouse stays! Love, honor, and cherish your spouse as your one constant person from the "I do's" to the last breath, and see how the family unit thrives when that relationship is cultivated and valued.

Chapter 6

Check in Regularly

Checking in with one another is the C that enables you to keep your finger on the pulse of your marriage. As routine medical checkups are necessary for the health and maintenance of your physical body, so is regularly checking in with your spouse for the health and maintenance of your most valued relationship. This C is where you both determine whether your plans are working the way you both had hoped, or whether you need to collaborate on a new plan of action.

It's good to hold an image of what you want your relationship to ultimately look like. Remember when I shared that disappointment is found in the gap between your expectations and reality? How you close that gap, and how often, makes all the difference. The gap happens in every marriage, even if you were intentional to set expectations at the beginning of your marriage. There's no way of seeing exactly how your life will play out until you experience it in real time. It's also normal when the areas where you used to be strong slip into a pattern that no longer works. We all get lazy or busy or distracted and realize at some point that things have grown stale or regularly combative. Anyone who has a healthy, lifelong marriage has been there—even several times, let me assure you. Unmet expectations can really break the flow of a healthy relationship if we don't take the time to honestly address situations that have wounded us or caused us to feel unappreciated, unloved, misunderstood, or unnoticed. These feelings can grow to feel insurmountable quickly. Because this is normal, it is imperative that we check in regularly to gauge where we both are at in the health of the merge.

Planned Check-Ins

Checking in regularly is imperative to keeping your rock pile low to nonexistent. The goal is to not allow a bunch of little unresolved issues to become a divisive rock wall between you and your spouse. It takes guts to do the right, hard thing regularly. It takes tenacity to stay with the issues until you get to the root of the problem. It takes wisdom and discernment to pick your battles: learning to distinguish true issues from little annoyances that you can let go, and discovering the symptoms of a difference in opinion versus a larger issue that needs to be addressed. In our home we call it "majoring on the majors and minoring on the minors." Guess what? It takes time for all of us to become more aware of self, learn about triggers and why they're there, and then expand that to awareness of your spouse. That awareness also includes what his or her triggers are, where they originated from, and the emotions that are tightly knit to his/her responses to those triggers. When we merge our lives with someone else for life, we are committing to truly opening ourselves up regularly to one other person, exposing the good, the bad, and the hard to live with, for the purpose of growing together into a more collaborative, loving, lifelong rhythm.

We encourage you to check in regularly to begin tweaking the process, so your process is custom-made for the two of you. No two marriages look the same, so this will consist of you taking a basic framework of marriage, and quite literally custom designing what you want it to look like and how it will play out. That's what the check-in is all about. Asking, "How is this working for you?" and "How can we make this better?" We all have perks and quirks, those hidden things that show up as we live with someone day in and day out over a lifetime. Things we didn't see (or chose to overlook) until we were married and began setting up our family; both the surprisingly good (perks) and oddly annoying (quirks). Every person has them, and they are a normal part of the lifelong discovery of merging your life with someone else.

What sounds good in conversation, or on paper, or even in a book, often plays out quite differently with all the nuances that each of your personalities, experiences, and individual perks and quirks bring to the equation. When you build conversation into your daily patterns by delegating regular time together, space is created for you to learn how to navigate all the little ways that you've now merged your lives.

Marriage really is fun, frustrating, and wonderful all rolled into one amazing adventure! Why would we think it wouldn't be? When we make the time to know ourselves, and know our partner, and to love one another enough to settle in and do the work of growing together, it really does create the framework for a healthy relationship that keeps a clean record with one another and allows you to have fun together!

> Every person desires to be deeply known by another person, and accepted and loved.

Every person desires to be deeply known by another person, and accepted and loved. When we feel known, accepted, and loved we begin to blossom personally, to grow together with our spouse, trusting that our person won't leave when it gets hard or when we are unlikable. When we feel safe, we are more open to grow within our most trusted relationship. If this concept is foreign to you, you might be thinking this sounds risky. You would be right. We do risk when we choose to trust someone after we've been hurt, let down, or even left in our past experiences. If we're honest, at some point we have let others down as well. The goal isn't to find a perfect person who will never let us down, but someone who will help us mend things afterward. Someone to ask forgiveness from and who will offer it to us as well, regularly.

The strength of a marriage that will last a lifetime is dependent on each of you risking being hurt to give the intimacy of marriage a fighting chance. The truth is, there are no guarantees that any marriage will go the distance. Marriage is a risk, which is why we want to treat it with the respect and attentiveness that the most cherished relationship we'll ever be a part of requires and deserves. Because its also risky to *not* ever give ourselves and our spouse the chance to create the kind of intimacy that only lifelong marriage provides. As human beings we are designed for relationships, to crave a deep connection where we are seen, valued, and allowed to grow. Life is far more meaningful when we walk side by side for life with the same person, so while the stakes are high, what we get in return makes the risk worthwhile. Every person in every marriage must decide which is the bigger risk: opening yourself up fully to your spouse and risking being hurt or misunderstood, or holding back parts of yourself, never fully giving yourself or your marriage a chance to grow in the intimacy of full disclosure.

Understanding is a beautiful gift you can work to give to one another. Once you understand your spouse, you are far more apt to trust and rely on their motives and even their perspective. You begin to know how best to speak to one another in a way that you each truly hear what the other person is saying, and feel heard as well. At its root, marriage is committing to grow with your person more intimately than with anyone else on this earth. That initial promise grows as every day we choose to nurture that love, even as our spouse begins to see all the parts of ourselves that we don't lead with.

If you skip the early steps of taking the assessment and reading about yourself and your spouse, you may be kept in the dark about what really makes you and your person tick. You may find yourself in the same patterns of not understanding one another. I should know. It was years before KC and I figured each other out through sheer trial and error, and through a lot of misunderstandings, misreading one another, and wrong assumptions. But we stayed committed and kept checking in on what the other's experience was, tweaking, and trying again. Perhaps the biggest issue in my early marriage was the incorrect thinking that there was *one right way* to be for each of our roles (each of us thought it was our way—surprise, surprise) and that the other person was either being stubborn or unwilling to really see what the other saw. It might seem silly to you, but when we read that we were wired differently, and that our differences actually made us better as a couple, we were finally able to allow ourselves and one another to lean into becoming our best selves. No longer did we try to get one another to see like, think like, respond like us; we were free to become who we were created to be. What beautiful freedom!

If this is new for you, and if you know yourself well enough to know that your personality resists conflict, then you might be tempted to think that this whole topic feels too confrontational, and you'd rather not go there. Or maybe you feel the need to tell yourself to "suck it up" and ignore whatever is bothering or hurting you, to just deal with it internally. It may be underground, but you are building a rock wall when you push things down that bother you for the sake of keeping the peace. That rock pile is growing whether you want it to or not. Problems left unsolved, hurts left unaddressed, and differences pushed down will pile up somewhere within. Eventually, you'll be required to address them in some way, usually in a dysfunctional way. Keeping the peace might sound calm, but there's a storm a-brewin'.

The opposite end of the spectrum is that you may feel the need to address every little thing, compounded by bringing up past situations that support your case, entering into the conversation verbally swinging. This gives you an internal solid case against your partner, proving to you and to anyone with reasoning that your spouse really is . . . whatever label you've put on them: selfish, distant, stubborn, etc.

We've heard all of these and more in marriage mentoring over the years. You, and only you can decide if you want to *be* right, or if you want to *make things right*. If you're inclined to ignore problems, it's easy to convince yourself that you're keeping the peace, rather than addressing the issues in a healthy, open way that makes peace where there currently isn't. The truth is, your feelings are valid, and there is probably a pattern you're stuck in, whether spoken or unspoken, which has the potential to leave you feeling unseen or uncared for. In actuality, a number of other real-life distractions may need a scheduled check-in to see how you're both doing. This can be daily (recommended) or weekly, but regular check-ins are what will keep your rock pile small and your relationship growing and healthy.

Perhaps your story is similar to ours. When KC and I were dating and engaged we would talk for hours about everything. Truly. We look back and wonder how we got up every morning for work and school, because we would talk till four in the morning. Sure, there was probably some kissing in there too, but we really talked a lot. Weekday, weekend, we talked about every detail of every subject that came to mind, into the wee hours of the morning. Then we'd both get up at six the next morning, go to school or work, and repeat that same pattern the next night. I think we literally lived on love and the excitement that came from discovering one another's thoughts, ideas, past mistakes and future hopes and plans. Those nights of talking are my favorite memories from the early days.

And then we got married. And we didn't have to say goodnight and leave one another. We got to stay the night. Every night! It was so fun, but I can tell you that now, having been married for thirty-one-plus years, we have not stayed up talking until 4 A.M. once since. Ha! It's not like we intentionally pulled a bait and switch; but once we were married, that sense of urgency to be together and discover all the wonderful things about one another transitioned to a more stable, sustainable schedule as we merged our relationship amongst our schedules, bills, and responsibilities. We suddenly didn't have to arrange time to be together apart from those things. It was such fun to now get to live together as husband and wife, coming home from school or work to the same place, but we quickly fell into some new habits that didn't serve our new marriage well. There were some real adjustments to be made, specifically about how we spent the time we were together. (Including paying some missed overdue bills that had been casualties of our "living on love" season.)

Before we were married, we used to rush home, freshen up to see each other, quickly take care of whatever individual home business absolutely had to be done, and rush out the door to see one another. Now, when we came home, we greeted one another happily and I'd set to work getting dinner ready and getting a workout in, while KC would stretch and go for a run. Then we'd use the evening to get caught up on the business at home and prepping for school and work the next day. It's just a normal and necessary part of life once we were married, and because time is short, we had to make time to intentionally be together. Not just in the same room or same home, but connecting through interaction and keeping up with one another's lives. It seems like it would be a no-brainer, but once you're married, you'll need to make a conscious effort to spend time together daily. It's easy to think that living together or being in the same space is equal to spending time together. It's not. It becomes very important to intentionally stay connected by making time spent together a daily priority after the wedding.

After the wedding, we combined our finances and bills together and created a singular budget; the pre-wedding dinner dates were now impractical for our new budget we made to save for our future plans. That time of courting was for a season, but was not sustainable if we wanted to buy a home, have me stay home with the kids once we had them, and begin to have a savings account. So we made some agreements based on outcomes that we chose together (the first C), alongside a plan detailing how to make that work.

For instance, when we were dating, the future together was a beautiful, romanticized dream. A dream of what was to come, of how our love would create the most wonderful of environments for love and nurturing both for us, and for our kids one day. The dream of becoming all that we felt we were created by God to be. It was romantic, and it was a beautiful vision for our future. In the practical world of marriage and life, that dream could only be accomplished as we worked together to define what we wanted, communicated clearly with one another, and collaborated on a plan for how we'd get to where we wanted to be. When we committed to the plan, that didn't necessarily mean it was going to play out exactly in real life as it did in the dreamy plan in our minds. The same will be for you. The dream is free, the journey isn't. It would cost us to go after what we dreamt of. It will cost you too. But that's part of laying down what we want in the now for what we want long term. Mentally prepare for it to need some "massaging." Regular check-ins become a critical step for making the plan fit your lives.

There are two versions of the check-in: daily, engaged, interested conversation to stay connected to your spouse as you have dinner together, or sitting on the couch after work rather than scrolling mindlessly on your phone or turning on the TV. You stoke the fires of deep connection as you share your life, both the challenging and interesting or noteworthy details of your day. Schedule time together to share what's on your mind and heart, a time for both people to feel seen, valued, heard, and cared for. For many, this comes naturally, but not necessarily for everyone. The daily check-in is a step you can immediately implement if it's not already a natural part of your relationship, in order to begin (re)creating that one-of-a-kind connection. As this is a relationship and not a business partnership, these conversations don't have to be planned out on an itinerary, though there's nothing wrong with that if you that's what it takes to get you in the habit of talking. Author of *Atomic Habits* James Clear says this about the daily habits we create around the things we desire for our lives and for our marriage: "Every action you take is a vote for the type of person you wish to become. No single instance will transform your beliefs, but as the votes build up, so does the evidence of your new identity."[18] In this case, the identity of your marriage.

The other version of the check-in is intentional, undistracted, planned-out time when you sit down to share about some of the bigger plans you collaborated on, the more comprehensive qualities you wanted for your marriage. I wouldn't recommend this being a regular part of your date nights, but it could be occasionally. You want to create fun, romantic memories with one another regularly without turning every date night into a meeting you eventually might dread. We made these conversations happen during road trips, undistracted stretches of time when we could talk for hours and then sit with what we'd discussed a little. This gave us the gift of undistracted time to process together as the road stretched out before us, keeping us present and engaged more easily. Obviously we weren't taking long drives but a few times a year, so the more regular check-ins happened on morning or evening walks or sitting out on our back porch swing on the weekend.

Then we started having children. As those kids grew, family time, birthday parties, and eventually weekend sports took much of the time we previously spent connecting on weekends. It's a classic example of collaboring on a plan and new life circumstances interrupting that plan. This made our carved-out time to talk about anything more of a challenge. The same will happen for you, whether it be kids, a new job, a new commitment in your community, or maybe you just grew tired of the same routines and chose to shake it up a bit. It's said that the one constant in life is change. When we understand that change is a normal part of life, even though we won't know what it looks like, then we'll be more attentive and intentional to adjust to the new norm and create a new plan to check in regularly to stay connected. This is putting boundaries around our most important relationship. By the time kids came into our story, we'd already made our check-ins a part of our marriage culture. That meant we had to get creative in making new space for us during the special but needy season of babies and toddlers. We've done that in every new season of life, and it has served us well. It will serve you well too.

Recently, we've moved from our home state of sunny California to the beautiful foothills of the world-renowned rocky mountains of Colorado. It was a life-changing move in many ways, but one of the biggest changes is that KC now works from home. Our home offices are separated by a short walk down the hallway. For the thirty years prior to that, he commuted through Los Angeles traffic about an hour each way daily to his office. For years I had a vision of KC working from home with me, so it was a dream come true when it came to be. In our new environment, my work looks pretty much the same, but KC now works just down the hall from me instead of an hour-and-a-half commute away. (I can hear him on a conference call as I type this.) But remember how the dream doesn't always play out just as it does in your head? It was great for me, no adjustment needed! For KC it was another story.

KC liked the time on his motorcycle to and from work. While he is not a fan of LA traffic, being on his bike is one of his favorite places to be, so he didn't really mind other than occasionally being cut off and nearly knocked into a nearby car. He'd had basically the same routine for the last forty years, and it was comfortably known to him. He liked getting to work early, reading his Bible and the news in the quiet of morning at his office, and knowing the defined perimeters of his work day. The motorcycle ride home mentally signified the close of the work part of his day, and as he pulled into our driveway it meant he was home, and it was down time. He loved the routine, and knew who he was in the security of it. And then we moved.

Now, with his office just downstairs, the lines were blurred between home and work. Everything he did was all in the same place. He was out of sorts for a bit. If you're an entrepreneur, that probably sounds appealing to you, as it does to me, but for someone who isn't, it really doesn't sound enticing. Every aspect of our lives had changed overnight, messing with the linear way that he feels most comfortable viewing and doing life. As individuals, our routines were now different. As as a couple, our routines were now different. For the last thirty years, I had seen him for the first time Monday through Friday at around 6:00 P.M.; then, all of a sudden, I was seeing (and hearing) him all day, anytime! It definitely has its perks, but there are also challenges. We are navigating a new way of connecting as we learn not to step on one another's toes. Or ears. This was my work space all day for so long while the kids were at school. I was alone in my house where I can be in my head to think, write, create, mentor, and run trainings online. I like to work in quiet or with soft classical music to inspire and activate my brain. KC likes to blare rock 'n' roll music, and to sing along, whistling and tapping to the beat as he works on his computer. After more than three decades of marriage, knowing each other so well and understanding how the other thinks so intimately by this point, we have been checking in very regularly these last nine months or so to make sure we don't lose sight of what we really want for our marriage in the changes that have tossed us around a bit. Guess what? We have such a long history of practicing check-ins with one another, that while we may not be adjusted to our circumstantial new norm, coupled with the fact that our new plan to connect looks way different from our plan to connect back in California, we have grown closer to one another through this hard, but exciting new season. That is the power of the check-in!

Wherever you are in your marriage, don't wait until you are frustrated, offended, or feeling lonely to tell your partner, "I know we agreed to this, but it is not working for me. Can we tweak it a bit?" Maybe you agreed that you'd go tent camping every summer, only to find that you feel more comfortable "camping" in, say, a hotel with crisp white sheets and room service. Or maybe you made a grand plan to do something as a couple to regularly expand your fun times and adventures together, like joining a bowling league, taking up hiking or biking, or exploring together in the great outdoors, but then you found that it wasn't actually fun for one or both of you. When we lay out the plan or the dream, it sounds so good at the time, but many times we find it just doesn't fit us. Sometimes we find that we've mentally inserted ourselves into a photo we saw on someone else's Instagram post, but as we got into the car or on the plane to go live our own big adventure, we got snapped back to reality to find it wasn't exactly what we'd hoped it would be. Maybe you sat down for your inaugural couples game night, and your spouse's inner Olympian came out. What for you was a fun, lighthearted game went hyper-competitive fast and ended with your not wanting a second game night. You might be tempted to just throw the whole plan out, and that may actually be the best way to go for a while until you work some other things out; but what if your spouse really loves the activity you committed to? Those check-in conversations are so important to keep your finger on the pulse of how it's currently working for each of you, and what you might do to make it a better fit for both of you.

What we envision in our heads will take time, regular check-ins, and re-collaborating for a new version (or tenth version) of the original plan. And sometimes, we just have to scrap the big plan to start small, personalizing it to ourselves and letting it expand as we adjust to one another and how we interact in our process. So many times, KC and I collaborated on a plan of action, and each time we tried to execute it, it was a miss. Sometimes we just needed a small tweak here or there, and sometimes the new plan was not even come close to what we had envisioned. As in all things, knowing, even expecting, a clumsy execution is of great value when we actually begin to act on the plans we agree to as a couple, though it can certainly be disappointing, especially if one of you really loves the agreed-upon activity. By being honest we create a healthy space for open communication about those types of disappointments. The point is not to go for perfection. The point is that we are aiming for a close, growing relationship, which takes a plan and massaging that plan to make sure it meets the needs of both people.

Checking in bridges those gaps that will happen. The goal is for regular check-ins to become a part of your daily interaction, keeping a pulse on the relationship and keeping your protective shield around your relationship. If it's not working, go back to the drawing board to analyze what's working, what's not working, what needs tweaking, and what needs to be put to rest for now.

It's said that experience is the best teacher. Not true. My guess is that you've had lots of experiences that haven't taught you anything. I know I have. Experiences that left me frustrated or feeling like something didn't measure up to what I hoped it would. There's a remedy for that: evaluate your experiences to extract the lessons. Only through evaluating your experiences can you determine whether the issue comes from application or attitude. Both are valid and must be addressed, so you can move forward with mutual buy-in to the original or new version of the plan.

On-The-Spot Check-Ins

Sometimes check-ins happen on the spot because of a snag in the flow of communication and application. This typically happens when the way you wanted it to go didn't play out and emotions got involved. An argument brings things quickly to a check. The human piece of applying what we've learned is that we bungle it. Old habits arise, and we act the opposite of how we wanted to act, or emotion bubbles up and we respond emotionally. Or when our spouse reacts in one of those ways, and we immediately want to put a title on it, which might feel real but isn't usually the full picture. Check in first with yourself. Ask yourself these three questions in that moment regarding the situation at hand: *What do I think? What do I know? What do I feel?* I love the differentiating nature of those questions because if you are more emotionally intuitive, your brain may catalogue what you feel or think as what you know. Once we've determind what we are feeling and thinking based on our filters of the situation, we'll then need to ask clarifying questions of our person, as we don't really *know* for certain if what we think and feel is based on what the other person was intending. Rather than becoming assumptive, stay in the curious zone.

Remember back when we talked about the value of talking to yourself? This kind of check-in might reveal internal patterns that have snuck into your methods of conflict resolution without you even realizing it. Do you say things to yourself like, "He'll never change," "She doesn't care about me or she'd do what I asked," "He is so selfish," or "I've told her this is important to me several times. She clearly doesn't care"? These statements are rarely fully true and take the issue at hand toward a less productive path.

The truth is, we all have some selfishness in us. If you think you don't, here's a funny little test. When you take a group photo, who is the first person you look at to determine whether it is a "good" photo or not? And what happens if the photo caught you mid-blink, or not holding in your abs? We determine it to be a terrible photo! We all do it. Our natural tendency is to look out for ourselves, take care of our own needs, and take our own side, even when there isn't a side to take. *Same team.*

I'm looking out for myself when I want KC to behave or respond how I want him to, and while I don't think it's a bad thing to have expectations for how I'd like us to get along, we all walk the fine line between expressing what we'd like and being manipulating or controlling. I don't really want him to robotically do what I say. I want him to engage with me to find a new way. I want him to hear my heart and make changes because he wants to, because I'm his teammate. His person. And I want to do the same for him.

It should not come as a surprise when unforgiven, unresolved issues in the past that are stored away in our memories—not purposely addressed and healed—come out bigger and more painful with every new problem that pops up. It's not hard to create a case against another person; even the person we've chosen to love, honor, and cherish for life. It's actually surprising how easy it is. We don't even have to try to assume the worst oftentimes. For many of us our natural tendency is to believe or fear the worst. If we aren't intentional about NOT creating a case (or rock pile), it will eventually need to be addressed before we move forward. That, or it's the beginning of a path of growing apart rather than growing through what you're going through. Maybe that's where you're at right now? No time like the present to begin to connect with your person in a new, healthier way.

Why put off till tomorrow what you can heal and lay to rest right now? Yes, it takes work, but so does couple's therapy to resolve years of unresolved little things that feel humongous. That's a heavy burden, one that we aren't meant to carry. If we want something great, we've got to be willing to do the work and fight for it. It's a lot of painful work to separate your home and family in divorce. It's not easy assessing by yourself what went wrong while in post-divorce therapy, before you can move on to your next relationship. I have had dear friends go through this process only to find that in the end, the thing(s) they'd given so much energy to holding in is the very thing that, when addressed, set them free.

In our experience, and for the couples we've mentored as they grew through their challenges, one person responding poorly when checked in on is rarely the result of a lack of caring; it's more about knowing what is the right (hard) thing to do at the right (hard) time when it's needed. And then disciplining ourselves to *do it*. These pop-up challenges typically need addressing at the most inconvenient times, when we don't feel like we have the energy or capacity to focus on what needs to be said or done. In marriage, the relationship is always in process. You're interacting with one another daily, merging your lives, habits, futures, and here-in-the-moment moments, both when we feel happy and when we feel bored or grouchy.

There are many "self-first" moments where we lose the internal struggle, thinking to ourselves, *I know I should, but I don't want to.* Or when we've been too lazy to do the right thing by the other person and respond with an "I don't feel like it right now, even though I know I should" attitude. Or we get prideful and draw private, internal lines in the sand that the other person has no idea about. Words we say to ourselves like "I always apologize first. This time, he can come to me." And we wait. And they don't jump through the hoop. And then what?

I've done all of those. Many times. I can remember being so offended by KC for I don't know what, and I vowed that I would not go to him to address the rock I had against him for the sake of resolution. I told myself that this time he was going to have to come to me. He saw me not bending and assumed I was really, *really* mad, so he gave me what he prefers from me when he's mad: quiet space to process. He stayed out of my way, he left me alone to cool down. (This was before he knew this was a bad idea for me.) As time passed, the more wide open space he gave me, and my internal talk to myself got more and more negative. I went right to work building my rock into a rock wall. What started off as a minor offense that had ticked me off quickly escalated into my mind, building a huge case against him. I am still amazed at how quickly my brain can go from *That was an insensitive comment* to *How will we ever get past this?*

By the time I came to him in frustrated tears, I'd built up my rock pile into a wall that felt insurmountable. I nurtured my wound internally, convincing myself that he *knew* I was waiting on him and he was being selfish and hurting me on purpose. What a great example of how assumptions and negative self-talk can be a toxic emotional cocktail! It's why navigating conflict resolution by our feelings alone is a recipe for destruction rather than for seeking understanding and resolution. The exact same scenario in KC's brain went like this: *Uh oh. I offended her. She's really mad. I'll wait out her anger, and when she calms down, I'll apologize.* Look where my emotions led my thinking, compared to how pragmatic and uncomplicated his actual thought process was. At the time, it took a lot of work to wade through my emotions and get down to the basic application of practicing what we were learning about communication. Look at the huge gap between our experiences of the same situation! Both of us were trying to apply what we were learning about ourselves, responding based on assumptions rooted in how we felt. Both of us treating the other the way WE want to be treated, instead of what matters most to the other person.

It happened so. Many. Times. We apologized a lot. We forgave a lot. And with each resolved rock we learned something about grace and what loving someone through highs and lows looks like and feels like. Even highs and lows that we created. When we treat our emotions as facts, we get into trouble when reality doesn't meet unspoken expectation.

> Why put off till tomorrow what you can heal and lay to rest right now?

Building Your Root System

I've learned so much in the last three decades of living with this man of mine. Marriage for life takes a lot of work. Merging two lives together for a lifetime requires hard, consistent work if we want to make a good marriage great. Having someone you can trust, who knows you, is for you, and appreciates all the complexities of your journey is a gift that many people don't have the privilege of being a part of; they get distracted by that hard work. What you and I view as romantic at twenty years of age is very different from what we view as romantic when we are ten, twenty, thirty-plus years into a lifelong marriage. In the early days it's based solely on the things that make us feel something. Though these things have their place in the relationship, as time goes and the relationship grows, it goes much deeper and becomes more beautifully powerful.

Several years ago, as our family expanded, KC and I moved into a home with a bit more room and a large yard that had well-established, ginormous trees surrounding the home. These were magnificent trees. In fact, whenever anyone came to the house, they'd comment on the trees. The trees that garnered the most praise were the oaks, and that yard had five of them.

In California, oak trees are protected trees. That means in order to remove an oak tree from your own property, the homeowner would have to petition the city for permission. We were told that in order to even to trim the tree, we'd have to hire a licensed arborist to do the job. California really takes their trees seriously. Anyway, when the arborist came to trim our tree, he told us that the tree in the front yard looked to be about four hundred years old. Can you imagine? If this tree could talk, it would have wonderful stories to tell.

The limbs of this tree were amazing. They spread out gracefully and powerfully in all directions, leaving cool, sun-laced shade below. A "mighty oak" to be sure. What I learned about these oaks was so fascinating, I couldn't help thinking about how similar it is to marriage. The root system of an oak tree is known to be tremendous. Though most of it lays shallow in the ground, its roots grow in a massive configuration of underground tentacle-like roots, which become the source of health for the tree and serve as an anchor in powerful winds.

When an oak starts to grow but is still very small, there is a lot of unseen action happening underground. The sprout of a newly growing oak tree looks spindly up top, but underground the extensive root system first spreads horizontally to prepare to support the future growth above ground. It's said that the root system of an oak may spread to occupy four to seven times the width of the tree's crown.

The work we do in private is our marriage root system. All those little decisions and conversations in private serve as the anchoring roots for the newly married couple. A brand-new marriage begins creating an extensive root system below the surface with each private trial and difference navigated, anchoring the marriage in trust and commitment through collaboration and communication. Each small or large difference that you settle, heal, and work through together is in effect the new tentacle-like roots that will strengthen and solidify you as a couple. When trials hit, every time we effectively communicate our way through them, the marriage relationship is strengthened.

View those missteps and moments of friction as building a healthy, complex root system intertwining your lives together. A root system that will grow deep and wide. Settle into the process with confidence rather than insecurity as you build a history of healthy conflict resolution that will serve as your marriage's anchor when the storms of life hit. Misunderstanding and difficulties won't shake you in the same way if you have built the root system to support a lifelong marriage. Find comfort and even peace in the midst of it all because of the commitment that you made and continue to make. Every time you check in to make sure you are on the same page, even as you see that page differently, trust that you are building something massive and tremendous that will strengthen you and hold you up in times of real hardship, pain, or loss.

Lean in as you find fun, creative, silly, endearing, meaningful ways to remind your person as often as possible, "I still choose you. No matter how hard it gets, it's you and me. For life." This gives your spouse the confidence to be themselves, to hold nothing back in their pursuit of authentic merging, trusting that the marriage is a safe place where they can count on love and acceptance. And the same applies to you.

When I was young and we were figuring it out, I knew this: KC loved me and wanted to stay married. That gave me the confidence to grow and become a better version of myself, because underneath it all I didn't have a fear that he would leave me. That was very safe for me. No matter how I felt, I *knew* that he was in it for life. Such a gift. We had a lot of under-the-surface, root-strengthening differences, and it helped to have that security. KC didn't have it as easy for a long time. Because of his history with having had an unstable home foundation in childhood, as well as a divorce in young adulthood, he had an underlying, unaddressed fear that I would one day leave him too. He'd had trust broken in relationships in his past, so it took a long time for him to fully trust that I was in for the long haul. He didn't put that on me, he just shouldered it alone, unbeknownst to me. That may be your story as well.

More than ten years after we said our "I do's," he came home after his men's Bible study group. He was unusually upbeat and cheery, like a years-long weight had been lifted. It had been. He called me back to our bedroom and sat me down. With a facial expression I can only describe as freedom, he said with a big smile, "Babe, I have something to tell you. I'm all in. I mean, I was as much as I could be before, but I held back something deep inside of me, subconsciously waiting for you to cheat on me, or wondering when you'd finally leave. I feel free of that. I choose to trust that you won't leave me, and I feel like I can give that last piece of myself to you." For ten years we had checked in with one another, sharing how we felt about where we were, but one day he got deep enough into the soil to find a deep rooted weed growing alongside our root system. One that didn't have anything to do with us, but one that affected us all the same.

I'm grateful KC allowed me to share this private, defining moment with you, in order to show that sometimes wounds from our past take years to dig out and let go for good. They may be wounds we don't openly recognize or know how to define or access without consistent self-examination in a safe, loving, lifelong relationship. We are only able to address these kinds of wounds by moving through the 5 Cs with patience, communication, and commitment to the process of detangling unhealthy thoughts. True merging gets deeper and deeper with time. These tools help us dig into the very fiber of what makes us who we are and allow us to address another human as we heal and grow with them.

What if we'd given up before we ever got to that level of intimacy with one another? We could have. There were a few times when it was so hard to break through the old patterns of ourselves, or when wounds from the past affected our level of engagement either knowingly or unknowingly, that we definitely could have quit. No one would have faulted us; people would have assumed we were just another couple that couldn't make it work. And we would have missed out on experiencing the kind of relationship that a person can find only when they go through the lows of marriage and come out stronger and better on the other side. For life.

Your marriage might take a lot less time to acclimate to one another and build your root system. I hope it does! But even if it takes you years, the reward is a friendship that has no match when it comes to intimacy, connection, and trust. My best advice for the checking-in step is to do it like your most important relationship depends on it, because it does. Even if it doesn't feel like it yet. Go all in, as soon as you can, at every level, while asking your partner to do the same. You are building your own mighty oak.

Lessons from A Baby Giraffe

Have you ever seen a video clip of a baby giraffe? For visual context, take a second to look up a video of a baby giraffe learning to walk. It's not only cute, it's a funny illustration for how you may feel as you begin using the 5 Cs. I'm not only struck by the giraffe's tenacity to keep trying even when he falls literally on his face, but I am amazed that each time he tries, it's with a slightly different strategy until finally, he stands up and takes his first wobbly step.

That giraffe is so relatable as you start to take your first steps using the 5 Cs. Though you and your spouse might nail it straight away, for most of us, it feels wobbly and even awkward as we verbalize things we've perhaps not verbalized before. Don't let it scare you off. Go back to your questions: What do you think? What do you feel? What do you know? Then, when you circle back you can process with your spouse how it felt and what you're thinking. After you have the first couple conversations, life may happen and crowd out the time for checking in with one another. You secretly might be relieved. That's okay, you have a lifetime to work it through. Allow yourself a little space to regroup, assess what you might do differently next time, then get right back together to talk about it. If you don't stay on it, too much time can lapse, and old habits will sneak back in. After all, it is how you've been communicating for a lifetime. New habits take time to become second nature.

The truth is, the 5 Cs "work" when you make space to use them. Mastery takes time, lots of awkward application, and more conversation. By that I don't just mean talking, but listening too. Really hear what the other person is saying as you affirm them regularly in their love language. Speak life over your person and your marriage, and be sure to verbalize to one another as often as possible that you love them and that you're staying.

Make time right out of the gate in your marriage, or as soon as possible if you're already married, to put these five Cs into practice. Once you have kids, if you decide to have kids, the patterns you're establishing now will hold up when the family expands, and eventually will become a part of your parenting.

I'm so thankful we started practicing early on. In the early years, before kids, like many newly married couples, we were just beginning to discover our differences and had all of our free time outside of work to address them because it was just the two of us. I can remember getting into an emotionally charged disagreement on our way to our first Lamaze class for our firstborn. We were just two and a half years into our marriage, still figuring one another out, and didn't yet know how to table our emotions until we could check in at a more convenient time. We walked into that class thirty minutes late, and my face was swollen from crying. We'd resolved it eventually, but everyone knew. Back then, we bungled through a fight right before what was supposed to be many fun outings together: in the parking lot of a big family wedding or driving to a date night. Once, we had a big blow up when I was sick as a dog with a fever. All of those things happened before kids, when we could work it through no matter how awkward the timing. Even when the kids were babies, we were free to talk anytime we wanted when things came up because, well, they couldn't understand us.

For us, our differences went next level as we emerged from the baby phase, and our parenting inclinations started to really show how differently we viewed our experiences, personalities, and perceived roles of mom and dad of four kids under school age (remember, we had four babies in five years). It's ironic that as our family started to take the shape we wanted it to, our differences showed up more obviously in both big and small ways. This was when I really started digging to find out how to better understand one another. Because I'd seen good marriages, I knew it was possible, we just needed to find our way. KC, on the other hand, had not seen a good marriage up close, so he was a guy with a vision for family with no prior experience for seeing it work.

There we were raising kids, learning our new roles, being involved in school, in church, in the community, and trying to find our way in private conversations. Those were the best of times, and the most challenging of times. In this season we had to be very intentional about staying connected through checking in. It's worth noting that in the midst of all of this, we were discovering that one of our kids was developing what would later be diagnosed as an anxiety disorder. While it is miserable to have your child go through something that you've never heard much about, it opened up a path of discovery, both for our child and for us. When we started down the road to finding answers for her, we really started learning about the brain, emotions, and how people are different. It led us to answers for ourselves as well.

It's amazing how when you stay curious and seek understanding, answers emerge, available to you. I am so grateful for people who wrote books, started podcasts, and became speakers to share what they'd learned through their own studies and journeys. Those people were busy. They had lots going on in their personal lives, but they found answers that they knew would help people, so they set out to share their knowledge with hungry people like us who were in desperate search of answers. It's why I'm writing this now, because someone else who found a way illuminated the path for us. In a nutshell, it boils down to this: do you want answers? Answers call us to act, to change our normal responses and behaviors in order to create a life that's available to people who are open to growth. As you'd imagine, I didn't always lean into the growth or application of what we learned at the same pace or in the same way as KC, and vice versa. But again, that's part of marriage: understanding that your person is differently wired than you and will process and respond differently. And loving someone for life says, "I'm choosing to love you in process."

As kids entered the scene, we learned to set perimeters and to let cooler heads prevail, and in a way, that helped us to not let a misunderstanding derail the fun. It was a really nice change of pace for us to find our way; we'd pause until we could check back in with one another to discuss it when we weren't as emotionally connected to the disagreement. In real life, if you argue on the way to seeing a movie as a family, or en route to the team party, you still have to show up with a smile on your face because no one wants anyone dragging their private issues into a public forum. In those days we learned to table it until we could get alone to work it out. For us, in a lot of ways, that little momentary break in the frustration cycle actually helped us to approach it from a different mindset when we came back together to work it through. And many times, it resolved much quicker because of the event we had to get through before we could resolve it.

That said, as our kids got old enough to understand when there was conflict between us, we chose to collaborate on a new plan so we could find the balance of letting them see us disagree, but also heal it in front of them. Remember, I didn't really see my parents disagree until I was a teenager because they chose to keep it all private, and KC's parents' method of claiming the hill in a marriage-spat-turned-war didn't provide a blueprint that fit us either. We were charting new ground here, as most of us are in one area or another, but when it's important to both of you to chart a new path, taking steps toward learning new ways opens up answers.

Based on our vastly different backgrounds with our parents' styles of arguing, as we raised our kids, we decided to do a combo of what my parents did, as well as arguing in front of them and letting them see the resolution. Of course, we used discernment regarding the topics we argued about in front of them. If we did get frustrated in front of them, we made sure that, if it was appropriate or unavoidable, we walked through the issue for them to observe. Then, whenever we did that, we made sure to apologize and forgive one another in front of them as well. Lots of times, we finished the disagreement in private to hash out the particulars of whatever had popped up, but then we'd do a replay in front of them so they had closure. Then I'd talk it through with them later so they could learn that it's normal for people who love each other to disagree, and that it's important to remain respectful, to apologize, and to forgive the other person.

I realize this isn't a parenting book, but I wanted to illustrate that the messiness of the marriage happens right alongside of, and often-times right in the middle of, the beauty of raising a family. While the marriage relationship is separate from the kids, it's also mixed together in one big bundle of memories, experiences, and teaching moments. Marriages involve real people who take real vacations where real hurt feelings happen as soon as we get on the road, or step onto the doorstep of a dinner party, or stand in line at the turnstile to enter The Happiest Place On Earth. Yes. We've even fought at Disneyland. Let's be real: I'd be willing to bet most couples have. Maybe not at Disneyland exactly, but fighting during a happy occasion doesn't make us less human. In fact, it sometimes highlights our human nature if either of us have any sort of stress about what we're heading into (spending money is a big source of anxiety for many people).

Clearly, the older and more practiced we got with regularly check-ing in to troubleshoot, the better we've gotten at moving through the other Cs to get back on track. That said, even after more than three decades of marriage we still offend one another and have to go through the steps. The nice thing is that now, we can step into the back room to discuss and take care of it immediately (or as close to "immediately" as possible, considering KC still needs a little space to process).

Checking in isn't just about how you communicate in an argument or as you navigate differences in opinion or expectation, although it's certainly a big piece of being married for life. It's about the good things that you've chosen for yourselves to be intentional about—focused time together, taking a class together, saving up for a vacation, or perhaps a business venture. If for example, you've decided to save to pay off a debt, it means that you may have pulled your purse strings tight to pay it off faster, and it may have been too tight. Maybe one of you feels it's too restrictive, or maybe you're hungry because you didn't leave enough money for food. It's admirable to tackle a debt aggressively, but if you haven't had a date in weeks, or if all of your socks have holes in them, you may need a check-in to ensure that neither one of you isn't growing bitter, feeling like there isn't any room for basics. A good check-in conversation can help you reconnect and recommit to the plan, or collaborate on a new version of the plan if the original is no longer working.

Don't Shy Away from Hot Button Topics

You may have noticed that throughout this book, while I gave some examples from our merge to show you how we applied the 5 Cs, I intentionally stayed away from defining specific topics in order to bring focus to *the process*. Throughout your married life you will have thousands of things pop up that will send you to your 5 Cs. Practice them regularly and you will naturally begin to use them in any given situation. Master them, and you'll find your communication healthy and successful. You'll still disagree and misread one another, but you'll find resolution much more quickly. Like with any tool or skill, the more you use it, the easier it becomes, and the more your marriage is defined by healthy, productive check-ins.

I would like to take just a moment to highlight two unique subjects that affect every marriage in a powerful way that you will probably check in to discuss many times throughout your merge. While you will have many friendships in your lifetime that will fill different needs in you as a person (we all need friends), these two areas are exclusive to your marriage relationship. They can elevate your trust and commitment to one another when they are addressed and can cause deep-seated division if ignored. I call them the "hot button topics." Have you guessed what they are? Money and sexual intimacy.

It is well documented that money is one of the main issues that causes the most conflict between married couples. Not necessarily a lack of money, though that certainly can add to the problem. No, the conflict is a result of the lack of healthy communication about money. We've found this to be true in both our personal experience as well as with couples we've mentored. It's typically because, as we've found from a book we use in our marriage prep and mentoring, we all have different views of money. The book calls these views "money personalities."[19] In short, our money personality reveals itself in how we view the tool of money based on each of our personal experiences or beliefs about money. There is no right or wrong way; it only helps us to identify where we are the same and where we are different in our views, which will help greatly as we work to communicate clearly with one another on this hot topic.

You may not even be aware of it, but how your parents viewed and used money has a lot to do with how you view and use money. If you had very little money growing up you may have a scarcity view. That can play out in a couple different ways, typically a) hoarding, not spending any money for fear of running out, or b) overspending because the concept of debt and money in-money out hasn't connected with you. If you grew up in a family where your parents had wealth, you may have understandably but mistakenly learned to live as if *you* had wealth. If whenever you needed it, your parents provided it, you may find yourself trying to keep up the same lifestyle that you had in your family of origin without the resources your parents had. Both can cause conflict in a marriage, and a healthy, collaborative way of viewing and using money is definitely a topic worthy of discussion and boundaries for long-term financial peace and health in your marriage. Whether you and your spouse have different or similar views, checking in regularly on the topic of money might be contrary to what you feel like doing, but it will be the only way to really merge your financial lives. At the end of this chapter I'll share with you a couple different tools we use in our mentoring and recommend for couples. One is to identify your money personalities so you can understand one another better, and the other is to help you come up with a plan for your money together. As *Financial Peace* author Dave Ramsey will say about fiscal responsibility, "you don't want your money telling you where you can and can't go; you take the reins and tell your money where it goes."[20] As you get on the same page financially and have regular check-ins, you learn to navigate one of the most common points of contention in marriage.

The second hot button topic is around sex and sexual intimacy. I don't know how or if your family talked about sex when you were growing up, but I know that for a lot of couples it was not openly discussed in their families of origin. Whether you had a parent sit down with you to explain things and answer questions about sex, or if you had to learn from other kids at school, or worse, tried to piece it together by looking at magazines or pornographic websites, my guess is that most didn't talk about the difference between the act of sex and sexual intimacy.

If you grew up going to church as I did, more than likely you were taught that sex was designed for marriage, and that sex outside of marriage was wrong. Once you were married, about the only thing commonly taught in church was "keep the marriage bed pure." Meaning, don't have sex with someone you're not married to. I don't want to get into the theology of all of that, but it's usually where talk of sex in the church stops. It leaves a lot of unanswered questions. Questions like, what if you do have sex before marriage—then what? And, if your first sexual encounter is on your wedding night, how do you go from saying no and keeping your boundaries, to suddenly being comfortable in this new arena and expected to make soul-connecting love? Oh, the undue pressure to perform! There are a lot of gray areas, and many more questions.

If you grew up outside of a religious affiliation, you may have blurred lines around sex, if any at all, leaving you to interpret a lot of questions on your own as well. "Wait until you're old enough," "Explore your sexuality," "Get some experience," "*When* you have sex, use protection," or "You don't want to get married until you've had enough 'fun sex,' and are ready to settle down with one person" (read *boring*)—these are just a few of the whole slew of perpetuated ideas pertaining to the timing, exploration, freedoms, and performance during the act of sex. Have you ever stopped to think how these ideas are being carried from one generation to another? I mean, these are the same stories that were told back before I was married. I think it starts in junior high (or maybe sooner these days, sadly) and continues on through writers of books, sitcoms, and movies, people who probably learned about sex as junior high schoolers themselves. A bunch of people writing make-believe stories based on . . . what? Guessing? Is it learned from their own deeply rewarding and meaningful lifelong relationships that they fought to build? Without realizing it, we've taken on thoughts and beliefs about sex from lack of information and from media written by writers who are trying to figure it out for themselves. Hey, I get that sex sells, but do we want that to be the prototype for our own sexual experiences? Probably not.

Together, choose to stop focusing or even obsessing about the act of sex alone and instead focus on intimacy: the deep connection that comes from vulnerably opening yourselves up to one another and to a lifetime of sex *and* sexual intimacy. In this space we can release ourselves from the exterior pressures to perform, and find the security and freedom to explore and to learn about ourselves and our person as we get better and better at sexual intimacy, instead of thinking about performing or meeting an unspoken perfect ideal. The explosive, magnetic draw to one another as you begin a sexual relationship with your spouse grows into a deeper connection of knowing one another so well that it brings your sex life to a mind-blowing level, for a lifetime. The rich, mind-body-soul connection of having a lifelong sex partner is unmatched.

In his book *The New Rules For Love, Sex, and Dating*, author Andy Stanley addresses the difference, saying, "You are sexually compatible with far more people than you are relationally compatible."[21] Sexual compatibility is about physical chemistry and the act of sex alone, whereas sexual intimacy is about the act of sex connected to open, relational intimacy. The problem is, it seems like the only place where people are showing the "how" to having a sexual relationship is in books, television, and in movies.

Let me put it plainly for you. Sexual intimacy in your marriage is about opening yourself up and revealing yourself to your spouse, what you're comfortable with, what you're not comfortable with, and to do so in such a way that your sexual relationship is deeply connected to being vulnerable and teaching one another even as you learn. There is no "perfect model" of a sex life, only what you and your partner create together. Unshackle yourself from the incorrect belief that you are performing to prove something to your spouse sexually and instead commit to open, clear communication and regular check-ins about the sex life you get to create. In the Action Step below I recommend a great book for you to start with together. Read it and allow yourselves to detangle from old, incorrect beliefs about sexual intimacy and embrace a healthy, fulfilling sex life, *for life!*

Foresight is 20/20

I know that's usually said about hindsight, but remember our exercise from Chapter Two, where I had you visualize yourself as a ninety-year-old? Whether you have no regrets in your relationship as of today or more than you'd like, from this point forward you and your spouse get to decide how the rest of the story goes. You have the rest of your life to live with intention and clarity from this point forward. What would ninety-year-old you say to you today?

There has never been, nor will there ever be, a marriage like yours. It's true! You and your spouse are one-of-a-kind, and while many marriage ceremonies are similar, marriages themselves vary greatly from couple to couple. You are two one-of-a-kind people who make up a one-of-a-kind, once-in-history couple. Together, over your lifetime you will discuss and need to come to terms with how to interact with in-laws and friends, how to spend your down time, where you'll live, how you'll live, whether you will have pets, who will make the bed, how you will put the toilet paper on the holder, and about a million other little and big subjects. My hope and prayer for you is that you settle into the journey and practice these steps over and over again for a lifetime.

The days are long and the years are short, so while it may feel like a big deal in the here and now, remember that life moves quickly and investing in your one marriage over the course of your life is a story worth your time, effort, emotion, trust, and love. With the day-to-day decisions you'll make supporting your initial promise, you have the ability to change the course, or continue the legacy of marriage in your family line for future generations to come. Yes, it will take work, and there will be many topics that will come to light over the course of a lifetime in your marriage that you'll need to identify, discuss, collaborate on, and create a plan for. As you grow, you'll need to continue to commit to the process by checking in with one another as life changes and expands. The pay-off is well worth it.

You now have the tools to build the marriage you desire for yourself. You have one life to live; build something that lasts and that makes you both better human beings. My fondest hope for you is that you lay down comparisons and past wounds and mistakes, release them and trust your spouse to do the same. As you commit together to use the tools to stay and fight for what matters most to you, keep your eye on the goal: that ninety-year-old couple who reaches the finish line with a lifelong love story rooted in purpose, adventure, passion, and plot twists. And for all of it to have meant something.

These 5 Cs will deepen your relationship, your intimacy, and ultimately your legacy. Each time you pick up a tool and use it, your marriage—any marriage—will grow to function healthier. The Cs can assuredly alter the unhealthy generational habits that have been passed down and strengthen the ones that you deem worth continuing. As you make these tools a part of you and the relationship you hold most dear, the more using them will become intuitive, and the benefits will extend outside the boundaries of your marriage. These communication tools work no matter the relationship, wherever

there is commitment to make the relationship better. But there is one more C I'd like to share with you that connects the power of the tools to you as a couple on a whole other level. This C exponentially amplifies the work you do in a way that oftentimes left me in awe and filled with gratitude in my own marriage.

The following chapter is a part of my life and our marriage that I haven't dived into until now. It might not resonate with everyone, but I believe it is our most powerful tool in our marriage toolbox. I call it the *maximizer* of marriage, because it is both trustworthy and proven. I want to share what has saved us at times when we fell short but were willing and open to having our hearts changed. Never intending to offend or force a belief on you, I would be remiss to not include this C because of how it affected the others. If you are willing or interested, it's my joy to share the maximizer of all other Cs: *Communion*.

Key Choices

Your calendar is your best tool for getting regular check-in times scheduled. The temptation is to cancel an appointment with yourself, but don't let it happen, even if you feel like there's not much to discuss! Your marriage is a living, changing, growing relationship, and just like any living thing, if you don't pay it attention or nurture it to cultivate growth together, it can wilt or go dormant. I don't say die because if both parties are willing, with a lot of work and possibly mentors or therapy, you can bring it fully alive again, possibly even better than before. That said, the easiest way to keep your marriage relationship healthy and growing is to prioritize a regular check-in—and get it on your calendar!

Action Steps

1. Together, decide that you will make the time to check in regularly with one another. Schedule this out months in advance, so as other things come up, it doesn't get pushed aside. That said, if a wedding or special event comes up at your scheduled time, reschedule your check-in time before RSVPing yes.

2. Together, give one another permission to approach the other if one of you is feeling detached. Decide on how you'd like the other person to approach it (how they'll say it in a way that connects with you) and commit to not get defensive when they do. After all, though it might feel like a critique, and you may feel defensive, what they're really saying is that they miss you, want to be close again, and want to check in to see if you feel the same. That's why it's really important to share how you'd like them to approach you, when or if they feel this way.

3. If the hot topics of money and sexual intimacy appealed to you, and you want to dig a little further into each of them, here are three books I'd recommend that have helped countless people master their finances and bring their sexual intimacy to new heights! *First Comes Love, Then Comes Money: A Couple's Guide To Financial Communication* by Bethany and Scott Palmer, *The Total Money Makeover* by Dave Ramsey, and *The Gift of Sex* by Clifford and Joyce Penner.

Chapter 7

The Maximizing "C," Communion

Thank you for allowing me to share how the sixth C, the maximizing C, impacted our marriage. The other 5 Cs will help you in a very practical way whether or not you read this maximizer chapter and apply this C, but if I omitted it, I would be leaving out a big part of my personal life, many of the victories in our process, and what I wholeheartedly believe to be the difference maker in our relationship.

It's challenging to describe the power of this C to someone who doesn't have personal experience with it, but I will do my best without making it sound mystical or overly dramatic. This C is a committed relationship, or communion, with God. This C ties all of the others together with an intimate belief and understanding that God loves us and has a plan for our marriage, a plan to bring deeper purpose to our marriage and hope to those who have none. KC's and my own relationship with God started just as differently as our family upbringings, but both came as a result of us realizing that all of the answers aren't found within ourselves. We individually had come to the end of ourselves and knew deep down there was something else. Someone else. Someone who had answers that filled a deep yearning for more.

Before I share more about the sixth C I want to address something head-on because by this point we are friends and have been on a journey together with these 5 Cs. I know that people have all sorts of past experiences that may have made them wary of or distrusting of being in "communion" (relationship) not just with God, but with the people who follow Him. I painfully acknowledge that there are many people who have used the name of Jesus, the church, and religious institutions to wield power and control over people, leaving them wounded and with protective walls up. It breaks my heart because that's not who Jesus is. In fact, he came to free people from those things. On the opposite end of the spectrum, I have also found that some people use the name of Jesus to justify behaviors, making Him fit into a narrative they're creating as they go. That isn't who He is either. I'm inviting you in this private little moment, with this book in your hands to revisit this idea of who He is and what that might mean for you. What if what you've seen, what you've heard, and what you had come to believe up to this point was not based on an accurate picture of God? What if looking with fresh eyes at something you've previously made a decision about brought new insight, deeper under-standing and a more clear view of who God actually is, and what that might mean to your life and future? What if communion with Him was just the piece that brought clarity, freedom and purpose? For you. For your relationships. It was for KC and me. I have many friends and family members who don't presently have a relationship with God, and I want them to know God as I know Him. Interestingly, through asking questions I've found that what turned people off or away rarely had anything to do with God himself, but rather a distorted picture of God; either through painful or disappointing experiences with church people and human policy, because of a distorted view of God that was inaccurate or incomplete, or even because of an inaccurate view of themselves that for one reason or another caused them to discount themselves from knowing God.

I too had an incorrect picture of God as a younger person. I believed in Him, but in my mind God governed from afar, as a distant ruler. I didn't know how to get to Him. As a child my family attended a liturgical church. It is a nice memory for me, and I enjoyed attending church, but at the time, there were pieces that connected with me, and pieces that just . . . didn't. Maybe you can relate. I viewed God to be good, but old, strict, and disconnected from me personally, and found most of the teachers in the church to be the same. I believe that's common with teachers, authors, speakers, and leaders in our lives; some you connect with, some you don't. Even as children, if we don't connect to the person who's teaching, then there's a good chance we'll miss the message they're trying to share.

My childhood church experience doesn't include trauma or wounds, and my parents did a good job at setting a positive example of living out their relationship with God both in how they spoke as well as their behavior. I really did believe in the God they told me about at home and in my church classes; I just felt disconnected from Him. He felt like a historical figure; real, but far off, elevated, looking down from high above the earth, not really infused in my day-to-day life, other than somehow connected to the guilt I felt when I knew I did something that didn't serve me or others well. From my young perspective, I understood that God wanted the best for me, and that the way for me to connect with Him was to make the right choices and memorize a bunch of prayers and faith declarations. I did my best to follow the rules that I thought might earn me a spot in heaven, but I was far from perfect, and I'm a terrible memorizer. Even today, if you ever see me speak, I have to have notes. In my young interpretation of God from my childhood, the pathway to Him was through two things I wasn't good at. And by my own definition, what I heard and did at church was not connected to who I was away from the ceremonies and classes. The choices I made on my own time were completely separate from the time I spent at church.

Because of the disconnect, as a teenager when all the rules without a relationship with God got tiring, restrictive, and without purpose, I went my own way. I didn't rebel because I was angry or felt unloved;

I rebelled because I didn't see how to infuse religion into my heart and choices. I made more than a few poor choices, and I came to the end of myself. I just knew I was missing something, that it had to do with God, but I had no idea how to bridge that gap. Maybe you can relate. Maybe you see someone who has a living, active, interactive relationship with God, and you want it, but you don't know how. You'd welcome it if someone showed you how to bridge that gap or how to reach up or across to wherever He is, and make it all real. That was me too. It wasn't until I got a true picture of Him that I saw that He wanted an intimate relationship with me, that He was trustworthy and the one who could help me make sense of it all. I found that without me doing anything, He so desired to be in relationship with me, and He had in fact already built the bridge to get to me by having His son Jesus come to earth to invite me to know Him. The way to communion with God was simply to accept the invitation Jesus extended to everyone.

KC's picture of God was different than mine. His parents, my much loved mother- and father-in-law Betty and Sam, chose not to teach their kids about God, so he had no picture at all about who or what God even was. He knew that his parents were strongly against Christianity, and he didn't know why until much later, when we learned that in Betty and Sam's personal experiences, church-going people had wounded them greatly. As those offenders were the only Christians they knew, they represented Jesus in their minds, and Betty and Sam separately had decided that they didn't want to have anything to do with those unloving behaviors connected to that belief system. They didn't know those people weren't at all representing the values of Jesus. Hurting people hurt other people, and that was what happened to them, sadly. So KC was raised without any knowledge or understanding about God. The idea of it all was very unfamiliar and mysterious to him; He wondered, what did it all mean? In the end, it wasn't even on his radar. He'd been to a church similar to the one I was raised in with one of his grandmothers, but God was never explained to him, so it didn't draw him; it scared him. When KC was a young teen, his older brother Scott learned about Jesus through the Jesus Movement in the 70s when he went to college. He came home to excitedly share this with KC. His faith was very new, and while it was very real for Scott, there were a lot of details left out as he shared, which still left a lot of gaps for KC.

It wasn't until he watched a British-Italian series on television in the late 70s called *Jesus of Nazareth* when the dots were connected for him. Going far beyond teachings of morality, the movie talked about the personhood of God as our Father; the revelations that God gave to humankind that were documented in the Hebrew Bible of a coming redeemer of mankind; how Yeshua (pronounced Jesus in English) fulfilled more than three hundred prophetic declarations made over more than two thousand years so we'd know how to recognize him; and how this savior in human form was born and died to connect people back to an intimate relationship with God the Father. Before the film and without context, God, sin, Jesus, and salvation were all words that made no sense to KC. As he watched the series, it created belief in KC, but at that time he chose not to follow. There's a difference. You can believe in something, weigh the consequences of what that belief means for your present lifestyle, and choose not to act on it, not to follow. For KC, his newfound conviction wasn't rooted deeply enough in him for him to upheave his current way of life, so he mentally pushed it to the side to be dealt with later. It took shallow root in his heart, but wasn't stronger than what he cared about at that time.

In 1987 someone I didn't even know invited me to a Young Life camp in northern California. Young Life is a Biblically based organization that shows high schoolers what it means to have a relationship about God in a fun, interactive way. While the camp's games and activities appealed to my sense of adventure, I was surprised by the sharing in the evenings. It was like a light—an understanding—switched on internally.

As the speakers shared, I couldn't wait to get alone to process what I was hearing and how it was connecting in my spirit. For the first time since I was a small kid, I could clearly see that God was relevant to where I was at in my life, and I felt that He wanted to know me. I can't explain how it happened, all I can say is that it became very real to me, and I was finding that I needed to make a decision with this new belief. I came to camp already believing in God, but I wasn't looking to be overly zealous. And yet . . . my spirit was moved, I felt different, and I wasn't sure what that meant for my own lifestyle. It wasn't told to me, but I was sensing very strongly that I needed to make some personal changes, and I was deep in the weeds of what that might cost me.

Have you ever seen the movie *The Wizard of Oz*? That's been the best way I can describe the changes that were quickly happening inside of me. The main character is a teenage girl named Dorothy Gale, who grew up on her family farm in a black-and-white world until a tornado lifted her home up and dropped it into a new world of dazzling color. I'll never forget the first time I saw the movie as she stepped out from the black and white split screen into a vibrant, colorful, fully alive world of new and different ways of viewing and doing life, and every bit as real. In the movie, the world radiating with color had existed all along. She just hadn't experienced it personally. That is the best way I can describe my first real interaction with Jesus. My eyes were open to something entirely new. I now saw a whole new dimension of life that had existed all along but was unknown and unseen to me. I was increasingly aware that God was very near, desiring to walk alongside of me, guiding me. I felt loved, my eyes had been opened to view Him in a new way, and I couldn't go back to *not* seeing. I saw a different way, but I also *felt* seen, valued, invited, purposed. God became personal. I found firsthand that religious rules without relationship had been rigid. Vacuous. Incomplete. Beginning a relationship with a God who was for me and had the best for me was other-dimentional and deeply fulfilling.

In choosing to follow Jesus, I made the intentional decision to lay down running my own life which, in many ways, felt counterfeit and full of guesswork, and instead took up a life full of purpose and passion that I just didn't have before. A life of being led and choosing to follow.

I was only seventeen, but I'd already made enough poor decisions that proved to me I was no good at being the god of my own life. I had been selfish and impulsive, and my instincts were many times harmful to myself and my relationships. Jesus was the door to personal, emotional, spiritual freedom to live a life by design following a loving, highly interactive God. He made life, and I now believed He had the instructions for how to live it abundantly! Oh, what sweet freedom and joy! I was so hungry to know Him and to *be known.*

KC was a little slower than I was to make a mess of things in his own life, because it wasn't until he was twenty-nine and going through a painful divorce when he revisited the idea of inviting God in. It goes back to that saying about why people change: they hurt enough that they must make a change, they learn enough that they decide to change, or circumstances thrust upon them force change. All three happened at once for KC, and no longer did his lifestyle keep him from choosing to follow Jesus, as that life was dissolving. After making his own choices for his own reasons for more than ten years after first believing in Jesus, he chose to follow Him.

We met again shortly after we'd each made our own decision to follow, and excitedly shared our stories with one another of how it all came to be. When two imperfect, flawed people who want to live abundant, fulfilling lives put their lives and marriage into a perfect, loving God's hands, amazing things can happen. KC and I invited Him into our lives and chose to come into agreement with the plans he had for us. Plans to prosper us and not to harm us. Plans to give us hope and a future.

The pictures we had of God were distorted, and when we were both ready and open, we went all in following Him: attending a Bible-teaching church, reading our Bibles on our own time, sharing what we were learning, joining Bible study groups to grow with others. Because we leaned into developing our communion with God both individually and as a couple, that relationship influenced our marriage in ways we never could have created on our own, apart from his involvement. It maximized our efforts because it was our mind, will, and spirit connecting with each other and with God. Once we got past ourselves and running our own lives through our own filters, we found our identity in the God who made us, and who made the way to be in communion with us.

The changes were both big and small. I'm not talking about an emotional feeling about God, I'm talking about believing, trusting, and following Him to become the next best versions of ourselves. It has been hard, but it is at the same time life-enhancing and fulfilling. I've never regretted it one day. We've each made that decision over and over again, finding our identity in our lifelong communion with God for more than thirty years now. We haven't always done it well, but having God guide our lives has helped us to become more loving humans toward ourselves, to one another, and to others outside of our home because He first loved us and showed us what true, purpose-filled, sacrificial love is. Over the years we have seen situational and lasting changes in each of us, and our lives are infinitely better and clearer on so many levels. God has guided us internally as we allowed Him to, and we have grown closer to Him, closer to one another, and closer to other people as well. Often it was not just about taking action steps, but about who we were becoming as we took those steps, having our hearts turned to a deeper love than we ever experienced when we were set in our own old patterns or habits. I don't want it to sound mystical, but there were times when following Him called on us to let him change our hearts, soften our internal jagged edges and hard stances by doing things that didn't come naturally. We willingly did so because we'd committed to what we wanted in the longterm being more important than digging in to win in the now. How did we learn His way? We read our Bibles, His words and guidance for how to live a life designed for communion with God and others, and we invited Him to speak to our hearts.

Making that initial decision and beginning to learn and grow is a great starting point. Making the decision to follow Jesus and lean in brings change from the inside out that is not paralleled. By the time KC and I met, God had already done some amazing work in each of us as individuals, but there were also things that would take years to work through to permanent changes. Many things, like self-sabotage, selfishness, laziness, lack of consistency, lack of empathy, stubbornness, the list goes on. When KC and I began our relationship, we were both excited to talk about and share our faith and discover what we wanted out of life and marriage. But when we got married and began to build our relationship, we learned very quickly that some things—many things—that are hardwired from childhood are very difficult to overcome, even if you really want to change. Old habits, combined with differences of personalities and the way we approached things, stirred to the surface and made our first couple years of marriage equal parts fun and crisis.

As soon as our marriage adventure began, we saw things—and you'll see things in your marriage adventure—that neither of us fully anticipated before saying "I do." Saying "I do" changes things in the relationship, much of it amazing and wonderful, but not all of it easy. Some of it is just plain difficult to navigate. Yes, there is security and confidence after having your person make the promise to love, honor, and cherish you for life, but also, your guard comes fully down and your truest natures are revealed. There is a security and comfort that comes in marriage that allows us to be our fullest self as we live as man and wife, weaknesses and all, but also trusting that we will continue to invite God to reveal areas where He wants to grow us. While KC and I had discussed so much on so many topics prior to walking down the aisle, living together as a married couple was just . . . different. That's when the real communion began.

Marriage, Party of . . . Three?

We believe that God invented the covenant of marriage to show two complementary parts of God in one family unit, with a little of each in both of us: the nurturing, loving side and the protective, warrior side. And when we read that God says the two "become one," it isn't that we lose ourselves or our individuality; it's that together, our marriage is meant to represent a completed, complex, but human version of both the tender and courageous parts of God. In short, we learn more about the fullness of God as we grow toward one another in our marriage. For us, the marriage covenant is not between just the two of us, but with God as well, the creator of the covenant. As the "maximizer" in this marriage, God created the mystery math of the marriage covenant, where one plus one equals one. We knew from the start that if we were going to make it work for life, we wanted to invite God in as an active and interactive part of our marriage. Which also means that sometimes, when we can't get through to one another or are struggling to come to the same page, we go directly to God to help us discern His will for us by learning more about

His character and heart. We believe He desires for us to involve Him, separately and together through reading our Bibles, but also in prayer, open and daily conversation with God where we grant the Spirit of God permission to correct, lead, and reroute us whenever and however He sees fit, for our good.

As you've read, KC and I have not always been a gold standard for all to follow. Instead, while we are not perfect, we *can* say with confidence, "Follow us, as we follow Jesus." We have had disagreements in private that I would be embarrassed for anyone to ever hear, because it highlighted our immaturity levels at the time and showcased our stubbornness and selfishness. At times it's been messy, complicated, frustrating, and there have been times when I wondered how we were going to come out on the other side, on the same side. Those were the times we would pray, asking God to give us direction. We would pray and seek God's will, rather than trying to bend or manipulate the situation for our own wills. I would open my heart to see what I could do to initiate reconcilation. There are times when I have compromised for peace, apologizing first, and times when KC has compromised for peace and apologized first.

While we've not always gotten it right the first go around, we have spent decades growing toward one another as our personalities and our weaknesses are highlighted in the process of two imperfect people trying to align their lives, for life, and try our best to show respect to one another and ultimately to the God who created this merging of two into one. We agreed to work through the day-to-day stuff to create a relationship that has grown and shaped us into something I wouldn't trade for an easier path, because our trials have shaped us into kinder, more compassionate, moldable, understanding, forgiving people. Our relationship was tested and our faith has been strengthened in hard times when we clung to the promise we made, when we asked God to change our hearts in order to serve him and one another well, and

> The same Spirit that spoke into our hearts is available to anyone willing to listen, to pause, to allow the interruption into selfishness.

when we learned to allow one another the safe space to grow. And the best thing about all of that is that it is not unique to us. The same Spirit that spoke into our hearts is available to anyone willing to listen, to pause, to allow the interruption into selfishness.

When we are getting along, I pray for KC. When I am mad at him and we keep stepping on one another's nerves, I pray for him, and I pray for myself to love him well. I want God's best for him, and if I want God's best for him, I will pray for him. And I pray for myself to be the best version of myself in spite of myself. I also pray for him to choose to be the best version of himself; this aligns my heart with what God wants for KC, but also acknowledges my understanding that the only person I have the power to change is me. And when I'm taking ownership of myself and allowing God to soften me in the process, my heart stays pliable, teachable, and open. It also is hard to be mad or hold a grudge against someone when you are praying for their best. And I do my best to remember that wanting the best for my spouse includes the way I speak to him, and speak to God about him.

I choose to regularly "talk to myself," reminding myself regularly of all the things about KC that I love and respect and admire. I prepare my heart to show openness to heal rather than attack or blame or accuse or gloat. And when I'm so consumed with allowing God to soften the areas of me that I can control, I'm less apt to be looking for his failings or what he should be doing. That's not to say that I wouldn't point out a way I'd like to be spoken to or treated, but once I've dealt with my shortcomings first, then I'm typically more understanding of his process as well.

I have learned the hard way that not resolving a problem as quickly as possible will only make it harder down the road to come to a resolution. I've learned that I don't ever want to give full vent to my frustration or anger in the moment, only to have to spend a bunch of time later talking about how those words wounded or offended him in addition to the issue at hand. How did I learn that? By giving full vent to my frustration or anger a few times, and seeing it blow up into something far bigger than it ever needed to be. I have been unkind, and I have been unbending, and I have jumped to conclusions more times than I should have. And by the grace of God and a willing husband, I have also been forgiven.

Mostly, in the areas of my life where I've learned big lessons, it's been because I tried something my own way, from a human perspective, with limited vision of the fullness of each situation. In spite of myself I have done the opposite of everything I have written in this book, and so you don't have to figure it out the hard way for yourself: let me tell you, it ends badly. Every time. The wonderful part of having God involved in our marriage is that He gently reminds us of a better way if we'll seek it through His written word and choose to act on it. He tells us how to honor one another as equal partners in our union, and when we follow that, every single time we have been healed and moved to a healthier place. So if you're like me and you mess up more than you wish, pause and quiet yourself to hear the still voice of God's Spirit reminding you of a better way as you read His word. When we practice this, it honors God as we honor one another.

No matter how much either KC or I have blown it, our end goal is resolution, so we have worked hard to tame our tongues with self-discipline. It's not easy; it's difficult. For me it means shutting my mouth when I want to use my words as a weapon, and praying for self-control to not blast him with words that are hard to take back, just because I feel like giving full vent to my frustration or anger. For KC,

I can only imagine that it was even more difficult to master because of his examples growing up. He's had amazing growth in this area because he wanted to grow and welcomed the opportunity. This has been hard for both of us, but we have worked really hard to master our tongues as we pray for God to soften our hearts. Thankfully and amazingly, He does it. Imagining that it was somehow easier for us would downgrade the hard work we did to deny our knee-jerk reactions, when we chose to follow that quiet, still voice inside. Our conflict resolution involves a whole lot of inner prayer, choosing to deny anger's prompts within, and choosing to love when angry. We both prayerfully work to intentionally be available to heal and resolve, to get in the mindset to forgive as soon as possible when forgiveness is necessary, to compromise when compromise is necessary, and to agree to disagree and drop it when we've both stated our positions. Sometimes it just boils down to a difference of opinion that isn't critical to moving forward.

When we choose to humbly listen and humbly speak our piece with a focus on reconciliation, even if we're both angry, we have respectful, emotionally safe conflict resolution. I don't believe that anger is wrong. Anger is a healthy emotion just like all the rest; how we speak and behave when angry makes it healthy or unhealthy. That's why in the Bible, in a letter to the followers of Jesus living in Ephesus, the apostle Paul, perhaps the greatest encourager of the church, says this about how we should respond when angry: "In your anger, do not sin." Anger is a natural human emotion. Anger is not sin. Rather, how we behave *when* we get angry is what we are challenged to control.

We believe marriage is so much more than two people just living together and owning the same stuff, merely hoping we don't grow apart. Relationships grow to become solid when each member commits to consistent, open, and direct communication. We are protective and offensive in how we protect areas where we have gaps in our partnership. We ask God to help us grow with one another. Just as we have used the 5 Cs in our marriage, we believe it is important to choose to come into communion with God, and from there, we communicate, collaborate, commit to the process, and check in with God as well. When marriage goes beyond a legal union to a covenant of three (you, your spouse, and God), regular communion with God is vital, as it maximizes the application of the 5 Cs with your spouse. When things are good and when things are hard, we lean into the creator of the marriage covenant, inviting His input, and we both choose to work for the greater good of the partnership. To work toward oneness as two very different individuals.

In times of friction in our relationship, I am encouraged when I remember that it's God's desire and plan for KC and me to stay married for life. When both of us intentionally choose to cooperate with this end in mind, He will help us to make that a reality. There have been several times when we have gone round and round on an issue, not able to solve it. I have prayed for KC in the same breath that I have complained about him to God. I have asked God to help us when we were stuck and submitted my thoughts to God's loving authority in my life, asking for His correction in areas that I am too blinded by frustration to see. Sometimes, I've prayed basic, primitive prayers, when it's all I've been able to spit out at times of desperation and frustration. I can honestly tell you that because we were both open to having our hearts spoken to, many times surrending my stubbornness and laying down my sword has been the way out of a war zone. There have been times when we used our tools in a clunky manner and found ourselves lacking, only to pause, prayerfully invite God in, and sense God's quiet, still message coming to mind, or a scripture verse calling me to love or show compassion or forgiveness. Sometimes mid-sentence, our minds received insight. Because we truly wanted resolution and were willing to listen and act on what we strongly sensed as God's input, we found our way out. Time and time again.

Today . . . wherever we are as you're reading this, KC and I are out living our lives following this same process back to resolution and marriage for life. Who knows? We might be working our way through a conflict at this very moment, but we do so because it's worth it and we've found God to be so, so faithful to maximize our efforts through communion with him. We have found, and believe wholeheartedly, that God's vision for marriage will have God's provision.

My friend, keep fighting fair, and keep fighting FOR one another!

If you have an interest in knowing God in the way I've described above, it's very simple. For more information on how to begin a relationship with Him, go to praytheprayer.today.

A Marriage Blessing

Dear Reader,

How I love you and want all of God's very best for you. I have prayed for you and for your person—thanking God that you found one another!

Each of you come from unique histories from each of your families. I pray this book will encourage you and be a resource to you in your marriage. You are creating your legacy as you create your marriage and family. You are in a long line of many who have gone before you, desiring to do the good, hard thing by creating a marriage that goes the distance.

Learn from the mistakes of others who have gone before you. I pray that the fruit of my mistakes helps you navigate your own. Build on what has been taught to you, modeled to you, for better and for worse; learn from the past mistakes that you have made, and let them go. You get to improve upon the history of marriage in your family line; do so with God's blessing and other trusted guidance and input. There is no perfect partner. There is no perfect marriage. Marriage is a covenant of two imperfect people choosing to enter into God's mystery math of marriage where one plus one equals one. You are two people coming together as one, with vows to one another and a covenant with God if you choose to invite him in. He is ready and desiring to help you.

It may be hard to imagine today, but there will be days when you don't "feel" in love. Or "feel" particularly loving toward the other. Love is a choice. Love is action. Hard days will come that will test your vows. Don't be surprised when they do. It's a natural part of the marriage journey that is strengthening your marriage root system. When you commit to work it through, your marriage will be refined in those times, will become stronger on the other side of those hardships, and over time your relationship truly will take on a life of its own, more powerful than you could ever imagine.

I pray you choose to follow Jesus and choose to believe the best of one another. Even when it's in an area not quite developed yet. We are all a work in progress.

Communicate regularly. Say I'm sorry and extend forgiveness regularly. Protect your intimacy, not just physical but emotional too. Don't let anyone come into that space that is only for the two of you. Not friends, not parents, not co-workers, not your extended family, and not even your children.

Choose your "team" wisely—your closest confidants—people who will encourage you to stay true to one another, even in the darkest of days. You are not meant to be in this life journey alone. God's word says, "A man will leave his father and mother and be united to his wife, and the two will become one flesh." When you say "I do," the two of you become one: one couple, one family, one team. Draw boundaries around your sacred new family unit and protect those boundaries. Give yourselves to one another daily and choose one another again and again. Know that there is a wealth of resources available to you when you need them. Seek them out, but be discerning about who you allow to speak into your most treasured relationship!

I'm praying for God's favor and blessing to be on you, your marriage, your children should you have them, and any future grandbabies to-be; for life. Though I haven't met you, I do love you, *I am so for you*, and I am praying for you to stay, to fight for one another, to forgive one another, and to make your own great, one-of-a-kind love story!

May God bless you and keep you!

Your friend, TRACI

Notes

1. Nick Morgan, "Thinking of Self-Publishing Your Book in 2013? Here's What You Need to Know," *Forbes* (January 2013). https://www.forbes.com/sites/nickmorgan/2013/01/08/thinking-of-self-publishing-your-book-in-2013-heres-what-you-need-to-know/?sh=35546aab14bb; Statista, "Leading Film Markets Worldwide from 2007 to 2018, by Number of Films Produced," (accessed March 2022). https://www.statista.com/statistics/252727/leading-film-markets-worldwide-by-number-of-films-produced/

2. Peter Velander, *A Good Beginning: Crossing the Bridge to Married Life* (Shepherd's Staff, 1985).

3. John C. Maxwell, *Today Matters: 12 Daily Practices to Guarantee Tomorrow's Success* (Center Street, 2008).

4. Florence Littauer, *Personality Plus: How to Understand Others by Understanding Yourself* (Fleming H. Revell, 1992).

5. Gary Chapman, *The 5 Love Languages* (Northfield Publishing, 2014).

6. Don Shula (1930-2020).

7. Simon Sinek, *Find Your Why: A Practical Guide for Discovering Purpose for You and Your Team.* (New York: Portfolio, 2017).

8. J.K. Rowling, *Harry Potter and the Goblet of Fire* (Bloomsbury, 2000).

9. Tony A. Gaskins Jr, social media post (April 24, 2013). https://twitter.com/tonygaskins/status/327150606294863872?lang=en.

10. Peter Velander, *A Good Beginning: A Companion Resource for the Premarriage Awareness Inventory* (Inver Grove Heights: Logos Productions, Inc., 1985).

11. Phil. 4:8-9 (The Message).

12. Melissa Michaels, "Make Room for What You Love," *Proverbs 31 Ministries* (June 2016). https://proverbs31.org/read/devotions/full-post/2016/06/16/make-room-for-what-you-love

13. World of Work Project, "Mehrabian's 7-38-55 Communication Model: It's More Than Words" (accessed March 2022). https://worldofwork.io/2019/07/mehrabians-7-38-55-communication-model/.

14. Andy Stanley, *Communicating for a Change* (Multnomah, 2006).

15. Mary Parke, "Are Married Parents Really Better for Children?" *Center for Law and Social Policy* (2003) https://www.clasp.org/sites/default/files/public/resources-and-publications/states/0086.pdf.

16. Drs. Les and Leslie Parrott, "Extended Conflict: 5 Tips for Overcoming a Stalemate," *Symbis Assessment* (July 2016). https://www.symbis.com/blog/5-tips-overcoming-stalemate/.

17. David D. Burns, *Feeling Good: The New Mood Therapy*. (Harper, 2008).

18. James Clear, *Atomic Habits* (Avery, 2018).

19. Bethany Palmer and Scott Palmer, *First Comes Love, Then Comes Money: A Couple's Guide to Financial Communication* (HarperOne, 2009).

20. Dave Ramsey, *Financial Peace: Restoring Financial Hope to You and Your Family* (Viking Adult, 1997).

21. Andy Stanley, *The New Rules for Love, Sex, and Dating* (Zondervan, 2015).

About the Author

Traci Morrow, mentored for years by John C. Maxwell, is the expert guide to relationships in his quintessential CLEAR growth program. She and her husband of thirty-one years have six kids and two sons-in-law, and they are loving their new role as grandparents to their first grandson! They live in Colorado with their two teenage sons, and on any given weekend, they can be found on a soccer field, or hiking or biking in the Rockies with their boys and their dogs.

About the Author